Honest
Doubt

JAMES A. HAUGHT

Honest Doubt

Essays on Atheism in a
Believing Society

 **Prometheus Books**

59 John Glenn Drive
Amherst, New York 14228-2197

Published 2007 by Prometheus Books

Inquiries should be addressed to
Prometheus Books
59 John Glenn Drive
Amherst, New York 14228–2197
VOICE: 716–691–0133, ext. 207
FAX: 716–564–2711
WWW.PROMETHEUSBOOKS.COM

11 10 09 08 07   5 4 3 2 1

Library of Congress Cataloging-in-Publication Data

Haught, James A.
     Honest doubt : essays on atheism in a believing society / by James A. Haught.
          p. cm.
     Includes bibliographical references.
     ISBN 978–1–59102–459–0 (alk. paper)
     1. Atheism. I. Title.

BL2747.3.H38 2007
211'.8—dc22

                                                            2006032646

Printed in the United States of America on acid-free paper

For Richard Dawkins, Sam Harris, Paul Kurtz, Tom Flynn, Annie Laurie Gaylor, Dan Barker, and many other thinkers struggling against America's pervasive supernaturalism

There lives more faith in honest doubt, believe me,
than in half the creeds.

Alfred, Lord Tennyson, *In Memoriam*

CONTENTS

INTRODUCTION

Consider this profound change:

For centuries, religion was so important to Europeans that they killed millions of people for it—in Catholic-Protestant wars, pogroms against Jews, the Holy Inquisition, Crusades against Muslims, witch hunts, massacres of Anabaptists, Hussite wars, extermination of "heretics," and other faith-based gore. Violent eradication was inflicted upon nonconformist Christian groups. "Blasphemers" were burned at the stake.

But today, Europe has largely forgotten religion. Attendance at churches and cathedrals is minuscule. Polls find fewer and fewer Europeans believing in gods, devils, heavens, hells, miracles, and the like.

In Britain, only 3 percent of people now worship regularly, according to one survey—and many of those are third world immigrants who attend talking-in-tongues services.[1] (A London research firm recently asked people to choose their favorites from a list of "inspira-

9

tional figures." Sixty-five percent picked Nelson Mandela; 6 percent named pop star Britney Spears; and 1 percent chose Jesus.) France, once a renowned bastion of Catholicism, now has mostly empty churches, attended by a few old women—while Muslim immigrants are France's most potent religious group. Italy, home of the Vatican, has the world's lowest birth rate, despite Catholic taboos against birth control. The same decline of faith is found in Germany, Spain, Holland, Scandinavia, and most of the continent. Even extremely Catholic Poland and Ireland are experiencing worship slippage.

British scholar Steve Bruce, author of *God Is Dead: Secularization in the West*, points out: Only 2 percent of Danes, Swedes, and Norwegians worship on a typical Sunday. At the start of the twentieth century, 55 percent of British children attended Sunday school, but by 2000, the ratio was down to 4 percent. In 1940, nearly half of Britons claimed to believe in a personal god, but only one-fourth did in 2000. And so on.

So a deep sociological question looms: Why did past Europeans kill for religion, but now their descendants shrug it off as inconsequential? Is this abandonment of supernatural faith another transition for humanity, like the past abandonments of slavery, colonialism, and the rule of kings? Is a new phase of civilization—the Secular Age—on the horizon?

Outside Europe, some other Western nations display the same pattern. Australia's traditional churches have suffered severe membership loss, while emotional, arm-waving, shouting worship has risen.[2] Canada, too, has seen great religious decline.

Ever since the Enlightenment, scientific-minded thinkers have predicted that religion eventually will die, because irrational thought cannot survive among modern people conditioned to seek logical explanations based on evidence. Recent scholars have attributed church losses to relativism—growing awareness that the world's many contradictory claims of divine certainty are equally dubious.[3] Whatever the cause, the transformation seems to be occurring in some lands.

However, a glaring exception is the United States, the advanced world's outstanding stronghold of religiosity. Supernatural belief dominates the US culture to a degree that baffles Europeans. Church attendance in America is much higher (even if poll findings are halved to offset the tendency of many people to assert greater sanctimony than they actually practice). Nearly 200 million Americans belong to 350,000 congregations, to which they donate $80 billion per year.[4] It's remarkable that America, home of spectacular scientific achievement, has such a high ratio of people worshiping deities.

"One of the most interesting puzzles in the sociology of religion," Boston University scholar Peter L. Berger wrote, "is why Americans are so much more religious as well as more churchly than Europeans."[5] A *Newsweek* survey for Christmas 2004 found that four-fifths of Americans think Jesus was born miraculously of a virgin, without a human father, and more than half believe he will return to Earth. America's best-selling books, with an astounding 62 million copies in print, are the "Left Behind" series of novels about a vengeful Jesus descending to destroy sinners.

Political life in the United States especially hinges on faith. Successful politicians invoke God frequently, appealing to religious voters. Accusations of impiety can be deadly against a campaign rival. This pattern has existed since the beginning of the Republic. In the 1800 presidential campaign, skeptical-minded Thomas Jefferson was denounced as a "howling atheist," a "hardened infidel," and an "enemy of religion."[6] Abraham Lincoln, who never joined a church, once wrote a long treatise against religion and intended to publish it—but friends burned it in a stove to prevent him from wrecking his political future.[7]

Starting in the 1970s, the power of fundamentalism in US politics rose significantly. First, the Moral Majority, then the Christian Coalition, plus thousands of evangelists, gradually swung conservative congregations to the Republican Party. The GOP became the new home of millions who advocate the "religious right" agenda: censorship of sexy movies and magazines, recriminalization of abortion, ostracism of homosexuals, imposition of government-backed religious displays and teacher-led school prayer, elimination of evolution from science courses, halting of stem cell research, curtailment of sex education, continuation of life-support for brain-dead patients, and the like. Oddly, this religious segment strongly supports militarism, the death penalty, and the right to carry pistols.

Republican George W. Bush, who underwent an emotional conversion, is an idol for this group. Without evangelical votes, he would not have been elected president in 2000 and 2004.[8] A London *Sunday Herald* writer observed dourly that Bush is "under the influence of the crackpot TV evangelism that is so peculiar to America."[9] The *Economist* of Britain said: "To Europeans, religion is the strangest and most disturbing feature about America."[10]

Growing political power of punitive-minded fundamentalists alarms various liberal Americans. Cornell University established "Theocracy Watch" to counteract what it calls "an ultraconservative religious movement seeking to impose a narrow theological agenda on secular society." Similar resistance to the religious-right tide is voiced by People for the American Way, Americans United for Separation of Church and State, and kindred groups.

A born-again candidate like Bush would be laughed off the campaign platform in Europe. Why does the United States harbor so much more religiosity, empowering such conservative politicians? Is it because this continent was settled partly by hidebound religious groups? (An Australian allegedly told an American: "We're the lucky ones. We got the criminals, and you got the Puritans.")

Still, even in the heyday of fundamentalist politics, clear signs indicate that secularism is rising in the United States, as it did in Europe. America's traditional "mainline" Protestant denominations with university-educated clergy have suffered great membership loss since the 1960s—while emotional, charismatic congregations have boomed.[11] Because of the mainline decline, the National Opinion Research Center at the University of Chicago predicts that Protestants soon will be less than half of the US population.

Dramatically, the number of Americans who say they have no religion has leaped rapidly to nearly 30 million. In 1990, the American Religious Identification Survey conducted by the City University of New York found that a rising number of US adults answered "none" when asked their religion. Researchers projected their 1990 number as 14.3 million. By 2001, this group had soared to 29.4 million—14 percent of US adults.

"One of the most striking 1990–2001 comparisons is the more than doubling of the adult population identifying with no religion," the study report said. This pattern is "completely consistent with similar secularizing trends in other Western, democratic societies," the report continued, adding: "The magnitude and role of this large secular segment of the American population is frequently ignored by scholars and politicians alike."

Another sign of fading religious power in America is the disappearance of church taboos. In the 1950s, it was a crime for unmarried couples to share a bedroom—and many states outlawed liquor clubs—and gays were sent to prison for "sodomy"—and abortion was a felony—and "blue laws" forbade stores to open on Sundays—and contraceptives couldn't be sold in some states—and Jews were banned from some organizations—and it was a crime to possess the equivalent of today's sexy R-rated movies or *Playboy* magazine. Now, all those puritanical strictures have been wiped out. Society progressed, despite church resistance.

And the loss of clerical authority is conspicuous in the Catholic Church, where millions of American members now ignore mandates against birth control and abortion. (It isn't easy for priests to proclaim what is morally righteous when hundreds in their ranks have been caught molesting children.)

All these indicators show religion losing ground in America—even while the fundamentalist bandwagon dominates politics and $80 billion flows into churches yearly, tax free.[12]

Among the 30 million "nones" in America, a cadre of activists feels a deep need to struggle against the nation's prevailing supernatural beliefs. They want to hasten the secularizing process, loosen the church grip on society, and make America safe for nonconformists. These include both free-acting individuals and members of crusading groups such as the Council for Secular Humanism, the Freedom from Religion Foundation, the American Humanist Association, American Atheists, the Ethical Culture Union, and a segment of the Unitarian Universalist Association.

In their different ways, they all strive to convince intelligent people that it's honorable to question miracle tales and that skeptics are just as moral as believers. They hope to advance the "freedom to doubt." There are several ways to press this mission:

- By appealing to people's mental honesty, the scientific mindset that seeks evidence to support beliefs.

- By citing tragic evils caused by religion, from human sacrifice, to holy wars, to persecutions, to the Jonestown massacre, to murders at abortion clinics.

- By citing great thinkers throughout history who have concluded that supernatural claims are hokum.

- By noting the obvious: that horrors such as the 2004 tsunami or AIDS prove clearly that the universe isn't governed by an all-merciful, all-powerful god.

- By pointing out the hypocrisy of church leaders who wear an air of moral superiority, then are exposed in repulsive scandals.

- By reminding people of past religions that died, whose gods now are seen as imaginary.

- By citing absurd church predictions and claims that flopped and now are deemed ludicrous.

- By asserting the need for separation of church and state, to prevent majority believers from using governmental police power to impose their beliefs on others.

All those approaches are utilized in the following essays that have been published in various journals. They are assembled in this collection to present the case against supernaturalism.

NOTES

1. Jessica Elgood, Ipsos MORI research firm, quoted in Dale Hurd, "Is Europe the New 'Dark Continent'?" CBN News, 2006.

2. National Church Life Survey, "Dramatic Shifts in Australia's Religious Landscape," 2001.

3. Among others, Pope Benedict XVI has denounced the "dictatorship of relativism" and President George W. Bush praised Pope John Paul II for standing firm against the "tides of moral relativism."

4. City University of New York, "American Religious Identity Survey,

2001"; Eileen Lindner, ed., *Yearbook of American and Canadian Churches 2005*, annual directory by the National Council of Churches of Christ in the USA (Nashville, TN: Abingdon, 2005).

5. Peter L. Berger, *The Desecularization of the World* (Grand Rapids, MI: Erdsman, 1999), p. 10.

6. Merrill D. Peterson, *Thomas Jefferson and the New Nation* (New York: Oxford University Press, 1970), p. 639; Helen Schachner, *Thomas Jefferson: A Biography* (Cranberry, NJ: Thomas Yoseloff, 1951), p. 640; John Ferling, "Cliffhanger: The Election of 1800," *Smithsonian*, November 2004, p. 48; James McEnteer, "Campaign '92: Form over Substance Once Again?" *Quincy, MA Patriot-Ledger*, September 7, 1991.

7. William Henry Herndon, *Herndon's Lincoln: The True Story of a Great Life*, 1989; Allen C. Guelzo, *Abraham Lincoln: Redeemer President* (Grand Rapids, MI: Erdsman, 1999), pp. 50–51.

8. News reports by the Associated Press, the *New York Times*, and other media in 2000 and 2004 asserted that support by white evangelical voters was sufficient to assure George W. Bush has narrow victories for president.

9. Quoted in Hurd, "Is Europe the New 'Dark Continent'?"

10. Ibid.

11. Andrew Walsh, "Protestants in Decline," *Religion in the News* (Winter 2004–2005): 16; City University of New York, "American Religious Identity Survey, 2001"; Thomas C. Reeves, *The Empty Church* (New York: Free Press, 1996), pp. 9–13.

12. Giving USA 2005, American Association of Fundraising Counsel Trust for Philanthropy; Susan Raymond, "Religion and Philanthropy: Prospects for the Second Collection," *On Philanthropy*, December 21, 2000.

1

LET'S OUTGROW FAIRY TALES

The supernatural spectrum is immense.

Gods, goddesses, devils, demons, angels, heavens, hells, purgatories, limbos, miracles, prophecies, visions, auras, saviors, saints, virgin births, immaculate conceptions, resurrections, bodily ascensions, faith healings, salvation, redemption, messages from the dead, voices from Atlantis, omens, clairvoyance, spirit signals, spirit possession, exorcisms, divine visitations, incarnations, reincarnations, second comings, judgment days, astrology horoscopes, psychic phenomena, psychic surgery, extrasensory perception, telekinesis, second sight, voodoo, fairies, leprechauns, werewolves, vampires, zombies, witches, warlocks, ghosts, wraiths, poltergeists, doppelgangers, incubi, succubi, palmistry, tarot cards, Ouija boards, levitation, out-of-body travel, magical transport to UFOs, Elvis on a

Previously published in *C-ville Weekly* (Charlottesville, Virginia), July 3–9, 2001, and in *Chicago Red Streak*, October 28, 2003.

flying saucer, invisible Lemurians in Mount Shasta, Thetans from a dying planet, and so on, and so forth.

All these magical beliefs have a common denominator: They lack tangible evidence. You can't test supernatural claims; you're supposed to accept them on blind faith. Their only backup is that they were "revealed" by a prophet, a guru, an astrologer, a shaman, a mullah, a mystic, a swami, a psychic, a soothsayer, or a "channeler."

That's sufficient proof for billions of people. Most of humanity prays to invisible spirits and envisions mystical realms. Most politicians invoke the deities. Supernaturalism pervades our species, consuming billions of person-hours and trillions of dollars. Millions of prayers to unseen beings are uttered every hour and millions of rituals performed. This extravaganza requires a vast variety of priests and facilities. The cost is astronomical. Money given by Americans to churches and broadcast ministries yearly exceeds the gross domestic product of many nations. (Lebanon, $18 billion; North Korea, $23 billion; Latvia, $24 billion; US religion, $80 billion.) Other investment is enormous: Americans spend $300 million a year on calls to psychic hotlines. Angel books and end-of-the-world books sell by millions.

Amid this global mishmash, I want to offer a lonely minority view: I think it's all fairy tales. Every last shred of it. The whole mystical array, from Jehovah and Beelzebub to Ramthis and the Lemurians, lacks any type of proof—unless you count weeping statues. My hunch is that every invisible spirit is purely imaginary. Therefore, the planet-spanning worship is expended on nothing.

I think that most intelligent, educated, scientific-minded people suspect that the spirit world doesn't exist. But they stay silent because it's rude to question people's faith. However, what about honesty? Aren't conscientious thinkers obliged to speak the truth as they see it? Aren't logical people allowed to ask for evidence?

Some researchers recently concluded that the human species is "wired" for faith, that our DNA includes coding for mystery. Maybe —but what about exceptions like me and similar doubters? Why doesn't our wiring cause us to swallow the supernatural?

Moreover, even ardent believers see absurdity in rival religions. Consider these examples.

Millions of Hindus pray over statues of Shiva's phallus. Ask Presbyterians if they think there's an unseen Shiva who wants his anatomy utilized in worship.

Catholics say that the Virgin Mary makes periodic appearances to the faithful. Ask Muslims if it's true.

Mormons say that Jesus was transported to America after his resurrection. Ask Buddhists if they believe it—or if they even accept the resurrection.

Jehovah's Witnesses say that, any day now, Satan will come out of the earth with an army of demons, and Jesus will come out of the sky with an army of angels, and the Battle of Armageddon will kill everyone except Jehovah's Witnesses. Ask Jews if this is correct.

Florida's Santeria worshipers sacrifice dogs, goats, chickens, and the like, tossing the bodies into waterways. Ask Baptists if the Santeria gods want animals to be killed.

Unification Church members say that Jesus visited Master Moon and told him to convert all people as "Moonies." Ask Methodists if this really occurred.

Muslim suicide bombers who sacrifice themselves in dismaying numbers are taught that "martyrs" go instantly to a paradise full of lovely houri nymphs. Ask Lutherans if past bombers are now in heaven with houris.

Millions of American Pentecostals say that the Holy Ghost causes them to spout "the unknown tongue," a spontaneous outpouring of sounds. Ask Episcopalians if the third member of the Trinity causes this phenomenon.

Scientologists say that every human has a soul that is a "thetan" that came from another planet. Ask Seventh-day Adventists if this is true.

Aztecs sacrificed thousands of victims—cutting out hearts, killing children, skinning maidens—for various gods such as an invisible feathered serpent. Ask any current church if the invisible feathered serpent really existed.

During the witch hunts, inquisitor priests tortured thousands of women into confessing that they flew through the sky, changed into animals, blighted crops, copulated with Satan, and so on. Ask any current church if the execution of "witches" was based on reality.

You see, most believers realize that other religions are bogus. Why do they think their own theology is different? I'm calling for the final step to honesty. If some magical spirits obviously are imaginary, it's logical to assume that others are, too.

The Western world is turning more rational, more scientific. Education is dispelling superstition. Unlike Europe, America remains a bulwark of churchgoing—yet educated Americans don't really expect divine intervention. If their children get pneumonia, they trust penicillin over prayer.

As for the familiar contention that supernatural beliefs make people more moral and humane, do you really think that Pat Robertson and Jerry Falwell are ethically superior to nonreligious Americans?

Polls find that the more education people have, the fewer their religious convictions. Therefore, the educated are the natural group to break away from magic. I'd like to see a revolt by the intelligent against myths.

Generally, the educated class laughs at quack-o miracle reports, but not at the prevailing majority religion. But there's no logical reason to consider one supernatural claim superior to another. No matter how much it's cloaked in poetry and allegory, religion consists of worshiping spooks—imaginary ones, in my view.

The time has come for thinking Americans to say, publicly and bluntly: There's no reliable evidence of invisible spirits. Worshiping them is a waste of time and money. Instead, let's use our minds to improve life for people here and now. Fairy tales came from the primitive past, and they have no place in the twenty-first century.

2

WHY WOULD GOD DROWN CHILDREN?

The ghastly Indian Ocean tsunami on the day after Christmas 2004—one of the worst natural disasters in the history of humanity—may have an unexpected side effect: Intelligent people increasingly may be forced to abandon the notion that an all-loving, all-powerful, fatherly, kindly creator god controls the universe.

If a deity caused the Indian Ocean horror, or callously did nothing to save the shrieking victims, he's a monster. The tragedy proves conclusively that an all-merciful, omnipotent, compassionate creator cannot exist.

Surely, after this horror, more perceptive people will see that it's bizarre to go to church and worship a god who presided over the drowning of perhaps a hundred thousand children and twice as many adults. Surely they'll begin to realize that the vast rigmarole of god worshiping rests on a fairy tale unsuited for enlightened moderns.

This same theological quandary has applied to many calamities

Previously published in *Free Inquiry*, April-May 2005.

again and again throughout the centuries. In philosophy, it's called "the problem of evil," and it covers a wide range of cruelties. How could a loving creator devise hurricanes, earthquakes, floods, twisters, and other people killers? How could he concoct leukemia for children, breast cancer for women, Alzheimer's for the old, and the like? How could he fashion cheetahs to disembowel fawns, sharks to rip seals, and pythons to crush pigs? Only a fiend would invent all these vicious things.

In the fourth century BCE, the Greek skeptic Epicurus was the first known thinker to spell out this dilemma. In his Aphorisms, he wrote: "Either God wants to abolish evil, and cannot; or he can, but does not want to. . . . If he wants to, but cannot, he is impotent. If he can, but does not want to, he is wicked. . . . If, as they say, God can abolish evil, and God really wants to do it, why is there evil in the world?"

In the twenty-four centuries since, no clergyman has been able to refute this ironclad logic. Instead, divines usually duck the question by declaring, "We can't know God's will"—although they claim to know his will on all other matters. (God's will usually matches the prejudices of the holy man proclaiming it.)

Primitive-minded people often think disasters are God's punishment for human sin. Some tribes sacrificed maidens to appease rumbling volcanoes. The historic Lisbon earthquake of 1755 likewise killed more than a hundred thousand people—and afterward, priests reportedly roamed the shattered streets, hanging people they suspected of incurring God's wrath.

Immediately after the Indian Ocean tragedy, Israel's chief Sephardi rabbi, Shlomo Amar, told Reuters: "This is an expression of God's great ire with the world. The world is being punished for wrongdoing." The international news syndicate also quoted a Hindu high priest as saying the tsunami was caused by "a huge amount of pent-up manmade evil on Earth," combined with positions of the planets. And it quoted a Jehovah's Witness as saying the tragedy is "a sign of the last days," fulfilling Christ's promise that devastation will precede the time when believers will "see the Son of Man coming in a cloud with power and great glory." Catholic Bishop Alex Dias of Port Blair, India, said the tsunami was "a warning from God to reflect deeply on the way we lead our lives." On MSNBC's *Scarborough Country*, Jennifer Giroux, director of Women Influencing the

Nation (WIN), said the tsunami was divine punishment for America's "cloning, homosexuality, trying to make homosexual marriages, abortion, lack of God in the schools, taking Jesus out of Christmas." She added ominously that God "will not be mocked."

What a bunch of imbeciles. Especially the latter: Why would a loving creator drown South Asians in a rage over American sins?

More sophisticated divines danced around the glaring quandary raised by the tsunami. The archbishop of Canterbury wrote in the London *Sunday Telegraph*: "The question—how can you believe in a God who permits suffering on this scale?—is very much around at the moment." Without answering the question, he noted that "belief has survived such tests again and again"—and he said the tragedies actually spur more faith.

(The archbishop may be right that this "act of god" probably will result in more irrational worship. After the horrible 1906 earthquake, the region around San Francisco experienced a surge in evangelism and growth of the Pentecostal talking-in-tongues movement. After the 9/11 "martyrs" killed three thousand Americans as a supposed service to God, millions of other Americans rushed to church to pray to the same God.)

Meanwhile, the tsunami caused some writers to speak boldly in places where religion wields less power. Columnist Kenneth Nguyen of the *Age* in Melbourne, Australia, wrote: "For agnostics, including me, the tsunami has highlighted just how unpalatable the idea of an interventionist God ultimately is. . . . The random destruction wreaked upon our Earth by one tectonic shift fits uneasily with prevailing visions of an all-powerful, philosophically benevolent God. Sunday's tsunami broke countless lives, hearts, communities. It would be little wonder if it ended up breaking many people's faith too."

And at Cape Town, South Africa, John Scarp wrote in the *Cape Argus*: "Natural disasters like this reveal the ultimate weakness of nearly all religions. . . . The desperate attempts of religion to justify them as part of God's plan simply reveal the delusional nature of religious belief."

Shakespeare's King Lear lamented: "As flies to wanton boys, are we to the gods. They kill us for their sport." But Shakespeare was speaking metaphorically. Privately, he had no use for gods (but he couldn't say so openly in his era of blasphemy trials).

Throughout history, some intelligent observers have realized that disasters are purely natural, not guided by spirits. Regarding a plague that killed a third of the people of Athens in 430 BCE, Thucydides wrote that prayers and oracles had no effect on the disease, and that Athenians who worshiped gods died as readily as sinners did. After an earthquake, forerunner to the eruption of Vesuvius, hit Pompeii in the first century CE, Seneca wrote: "Keep in mind that gods cause none of these things. . . . These phenomena have causes of their own; they do not rage on command."

In the wake of the horrible Indian Ocean tsunami, thoughtful people everywhere may see the absurdity of worshiping a supposedly loving god who, if he existed, would reign over the drowning of children.

3

WORST OF ALL,
IT WAS DONE FOR RELIGION

Amid the shock and grief after the 9/11 terrorism attack on the World Trade Center and the Pentagon, it was sickening to realize that the killers were impelled by religion.

Nothing except faith could make nineteen young men prepare for years, pledge to commit suicide, sneak into America, take pilot training, pose as airline passengers, then gladly throw away their lives, just to kill three thousand defenseless strangers who had done them no harm.

Handwritten Arabic papers found after the tragedy make it clear that the "martyrs" ardently believed that God would reward them in a magical paradise full of lovely houri nymphs. Incredibly, they thought murder was a route to heaven.

Almost the entire world thinks religion makes worshipers kind and brotherly. Nobody wants to face the fact that it turns some believers into killers. However, this other side of religion, the

Previously published in *Free Inquiry*, Winter 2001–2002.

unmentionable side, shouldn't be a surprise. It has been on display for millennia. Here's a brief overview of faith-based killing.

Many early civilizations sacrificed humans, mostly maidens and children, to multitudes of gods. The Old Testament records numerous massacres and executions by the ancient Hebrews, allegedly on orders from God. Even the first intellectual hub, ancient Greece, sentenced people to death for doubting the gods on Mount Olympus.

The arrival of Christianity supposedly was a step toward compassion—but the church bearing Christ's name soon began executing nonconformists and infidels. The Crusades were a series of ghastly wars against Muslims—and the crusaders warmed up for their eastward marches by killing "the infidels among us," Europe's Jews. Later, "internal crusades" were waged in Europe against off-brand Christians. This led to creation of the Inquisition, which tortured and burned the unorthodox. From the Inquisition grew the witch hunts, which did the same to countless women suspected of having sex with Satan, flying through the sky, changing into animals, and so forth.

The Reformation is viewed today as a transformation of Christianity—but it actually was a hideous convulsion of religious wars that slaughtered millions of Europeans. Along with it, the custom of massacring Jews, Anabaptists, and other unpopular minorities flowered.

Meanwhile, jihads (holy wars) spread Islam east to India and west to Morocco and Spain, with an uncountable death toll.

When the Baha'i faith sprouted in Iran in the 1850s, its followers were decimated by Shi'ite Muslims.

During that same period, the world's worst religious war occurred, but few Americans have ever heard of it. The Taiping Rebellion was caused by a Chinese convert who said God appeared to him, told him he was Jesus' younger brother, and commanded him to "destroy demons." He raised a holy army and ravaged the land. The war killed as many as 20 million Chinese, before the Taiping finally were exterminated by defense regiments, including one led by British adventurer "Chinese" Gordon. Deadly religion plagued Gordon. He later led an Egyptian army fending off Islamic holy warriors in the Nile Valley and was killed when the fanatics overran Khartoum.

Holy horrors didn't subside in the twentieth century. Pogroms by Orthodox Russians sacked 530 Jewish communities and killed sixty thousand residents during the Bolshevik Revolution. About the same time, a historic bloodbath occurred between Christian Armenians and Muslim Turks.

As for the Nazi Holocaust, numerous theologians have written that it was an outgrowth of centuries of Christian hostility that branded Jews as despised outsiders.

Three of India's Ghandis—Mohandas, Indira, and Rajiv—were assassinated by religious fanatics, as were Egypt's Anwar Sadat and Israel's Yitzhak Rabin.

Jonestown, Waco, Heaven's Gate, the Solar Temple, the nerve gas planted in Tokyo's subway—all these were religious atrocities. So are shootings at abortion clinics ("pro-life" murder) and bombings at gay nightclubs.

Horrible ethnic bloodshed in Bosnia, Kosovo, Sudan, Ulster, Lebanon, India, Indonesia, and elsewhere is rooted in the sociological phenomenon called "religious tribalism." Of course, these conflicts also involve politics, economics, culture, power grabbing, and other causes, but faith provides the labels dividing combatants into alien camps.

Thus the murderous side of religion has been clearly visible throughout history. Terrorist Osama bin Laden simply followed an age-old pattern when he recruited suicide bombers to shatter US embassies and facilities and issued a 1998 "fatwa" (religious edict): "We call on every Muslim who believes in God and hopes for reward to obey God's command to kill the Americans and plunder their possessions wherever he finds them and whenever he can."

After the 9/11 horror, bin Laden called it "a punishment from Allah" upon the United States. He added that thousands of other Islamic volunteers "have vowed for jihad and martyrdom."

Why do such believers willingly kill themselves in order to slaughter unsuspecting civilians? It affronts all humane values. The answer evidently lies in secret letters found later in luggage of the conspirators. The documents exhorted the killers to pray fervently to be accepted as martyrs: "You will be entering paradise. You will be entering the happiest life, everlasting life."

Just before impact, they were instructed to shout, "There is no god but Allah." Another section, translated from Arabic, told the suicide attackers: "The nymphs are calling out to you, 'Come over here, companion of Allah.'"

The nymphs are calling out to you! Good grief—the murderers

were impelled by adolescent male sex fantasies as well as by belief in a magical heaven.

Former National Security Council member Steven Simon, writing a book on faith-based terrorism, commented:

> This is not violence in the service of some practical program. It is killing infidels in the service of Allah. To a secular person, it's crazy. ... There is one objective here, to kill an enormous number of people and humiliate the Satanic power. There is no claim of responsibility because there is only one audience, and that is God.

Simon is correct: It's crazy. But no crazier than most of the holy horrors that have been occurring since earliest recorded times.

4

THE GOOFIER THE TALE, THE MORE IT'S SWALLOWED

W ell, the *Mothman* movie stirred thoughts about the eagerness of some people to believe nutty things.

Back in the 1960s, I wrote West Virginia newspaper reports on the original Mothman craze. After Mason County witnesses reported a "man-size" bird with a ten-foot wingspan and glowing red eyes, I figured they had seen a huge crane in the night and gotten overexcited. But the Mothman tale was unstoppable. Ardent fans didn't want an ornithological explanation. Speculation grew.

Flying saucer buffs—who flock to such bizarre happenings like, uh, moths to a flame—held a worldwide "Congress of Scientific Ufologists" at a Charleston hotel. Sponsors said a Philadelphia mystic who communicated with "space intelligences" foresaw a wave of UFO appearances during their session. But none occurred.

The ufologist meeting was held behind locked doors. The public

Previously published in the *Charleston Gazette*, April 25, 2002, and syndicated nationally.

wasn't allowed to hear what I assume were startling revelations. I wrote that participants planned to discuss Mothman and a Mason County couple who claimed they had been visited by many angels. In fact, the couple said they, themselves, had turned into angels. That was the last I heard of the angelic Mason countians. I wonder if they're still around.

The Mothman craze was similar to the much-publicized Braxton County Monster uproar during the same era—but I won't bore you with the 584th retelling of an eerie creature reportedly seen on a rural hilltop.

In fact, I was trying to ignore all such ding-a-ling topics, but someone sent me a book titled *The Abduction Enigma*. It says matter-of-factly that "between 3 million and 6 million Americans have been abducted" onto UFOs by space aliens who experimented on them. A Web site (www.abduct.com/irm.htm) offers to perform "alien implant removal and deactivation" for victims. The price is $65 to remove implants inserted in your body by "gray" aliens, and $95 to extract those of "reptilian" aliens. That's a bargain, when you think about it.

I'll offer a wager: If you concocted the most preposterous claim imaginable—say, that Mothman reappeared and told you to start a cult worshiping him—I'll bet some followers would join your movement and give you money. The record contains plenty of corroboration. For example:

- The mystic Judy Knight "channels" the voice of Ramtha, a warrior who lived in Atlantis 35,000 years ago. Hundreds of believers flock to hear Ramtha's revelations and pay up to $1,500 per session. Actress Shirley MacLaine says she wept with joy upon learning that she had been Ramtha's sister in ancient Atlantis.

- Members of the Heaven's Gate commune believed that if they "shed their containers" (committed suicide), they would be transported magically to a UFO behind the Hale-Bopp comet. So they did it.

- Some New Agers proclaim that magical "Lemurians" live inside Mount Shasta in California.

- Members of Japan's "Supreme Truth" sect worshiped their guru so fervently that they kissed his big toe, paid $2,000 each for a drink of his bathwater, and paid $10,000 to sip his blood. At his command, they planted nerve gas in Tokyo's subway to kill commuters.

- Armed militias out West contend that the Zionist Occupational Government (ZOG) is plotting to seize America for the Antichrist.

- Science fiction writer L. Ron Hubbard declared that planet Earth was an alien colony 75 million years ago, and that troublemakers were exterminated by nuclear explosions. Their spirits, called "thetans," became the souls of all humans. This assertion turned into Scientology, a billion-dollar religion that attracts Hollywood stars.

What does it mean that certain earnest, trusting people are eager to believe astounding things—so much that they'll part with their money or even their lives? It's baffling.

Personally, I've always admired pranksters who pull hoaxes to electrify True Believers. Such as British rowdies who sneak out at night—usually after a few pints—to make mysterious "crop circles" in fields. Or kindred spirits who fake photos of Bigfoot and the Loch Ness Monster.

Back when Mothman and the Braxton creature were hot topics, my cousin and I—young renegades—hatched a scheme. We had some brilliant reflectors that had been pried from posts of those old-time wooden guardrails along roads. We planned to attach two of them to eyeglasses frames to make gleaming eyes.

We plotted to hide among roadside trees at night, then step into the glare of approaching headlights, then run away—and wait for hysterical news reports about the glowing-eyed monster prowling the region.

We never did it—which is just as well because we might have caused wrecks. But I still relish the memory of our youthful scheming. If we had pulled it off, eager believers today probably would be recalling the mysterious visitor with gleaming eyes who haunted rural roads, then vanished. Who knows—maybe it even would be a *Mothman*-type movie.

5

BREAKING THE LAST TABOO

Few Americans know that Thomas Jefferson wrote in a letter to John Adams: "The day will come when the mystical generation of Jesus, by the supreme being as his father in the womb of a virgin, will be classed with the fable of the generation of Minerva in the brain of Jupiter."

Or that Albert Einstein wrote in the *New York Times* in 1930: "I cannot imagine a God who rewards and punishes the objects of his creation, whose purposes are modeled after our own—a God, in short, who is but a reflection of human frailty. Neither can I believe that the individual survives the death of his body, although feeble souls harbor such thoughts through fear or ridiculous egotism."

Or that Mark Twain wrote in his journal: "I cannot see how a man of any large degree of humorous perception can ever be religious—unless he purposely shut the eyes of his mind & keep them shut by force."

Or that Emily Brontë wrote in 1846: "Vain are the thousand

Previously published in *Free Inquiry*, Winter 1996–1997.

creeds that move men's hearts, unutterably vain, worthless as wither'd weeds."

Or that Sigmund Freud wrote in a letter to a friend: "Neither in my private life nor in my writings, have I ever made a secret of being an out-and-out unbeliever."

Or that Thomas Paine wrote in *The Age of Reason*: "All national institutions of churches, whether Jewish, Christian or Turkish, appear to me no other than human inventions, set up to terrify and enslave mankind, and monopolize power and profit."

Or that Thomas Edison told the *New York Times* in 1910: "I cannot believe in the immortality of the soul. . . . No, all this talk of an existence for us, as individuals, beyond the grave is wrong. It is born of our tenacity of life—our desire to go on living—our dread of coming to an end."

Or that Voltaire wrote in a letter to Frederick the Great: "Christianity is the most ridiculous, the most absurd, and bloody religion that has ever infected the world."

Or that Beethoven shunned religion and scorned the clergy.

Or that the motto of Margaret Sanger's birth-control newsletter was: "No gods, no masters."

Or that Clarence Darrow said in a 1930 speech in Toronto: "I don't believe in God because I don't believe in Mother Goose."

Or that President William Howard Taft said, in a letter declining the presidency of Yale University: "I do not believe in the divinity of Christ, and there are many other of the postulates of the orthodox creed to which I cannot subscribe."

Or that Luther Burbank told a newspaper interviewer in 1926: "As a scientist, I cannot help feeling that all religions are on a tottering foundation. . . . I am an infidel today. I do not believe what has been served to me to believe. I am a doubter, a questioner, a skeptic. When it can be proved to me that there is immortality, that there is resurrection beyond the gates of death, then I will believe. Until then, no."

Or that Bertrand Russell wrote in 1930: "My own view of religion is that of Lucretius. I regard it as a disease born of fear and as a source of untold misery to the human race."

Or that George Bernard Shaw wrote in the preface to one of his plays: "At present there is not a single credible established religion in the world."

Or that Leo Tolstoy wrote in response to his excommunication by the Holy Synod of the Russian Orthodox Church: "To regard Christ as God, and to pray to him, are to my mind the greatest possible sacrilege."

Or that Charles Darwin said: "The mystery of the beginning of all things is insoluble by us, and I for one must be content to remain an agnostic."

Or that Kurt Vonnegut said: "Say what you will about the sweet miracle of unquestioning faith, I consider a capacity for it terrifying and absolutely vile."

Or that Gloria Steinem said: "By the year 2000, we will, I hope, raise our children to believe in human potential, not God."

Many, perhaps most, of the world's outstanding thinkers, scientists, writers, reformers—people who changed Western life—have been religious skeptics. But this fact is little known in America. Why?

Because our nation has one last taboo, one unmentionable topic: religious doubt.

In the daily tumult, it's permissible to challenge any idea, save one. Supernatural religion—invisible gods and devils, heavens and hells—is off limits. It's acceptable to write that Elvis is alive on a UFO, but not that God is a figment of the imagination. A few "freethought" journals do so, but mainstream media mostly stay mum.

There's an unspoken consensus that the subject is too touchy, that it's "impolite" to question anyone's religion. In a nation of 200 million church members, with an upsurge of fundamentalism, too many feelings would be hurt.

Why are some believers angered by disbelief? Bertrand Russell offered this explanation:

> There is something feeble and a little contemptible about a man who cannot face the perils of life without the help of comfortable myths. Almost inevitably, some part of him is aware that they are myths, and that he believes them only because they are comforting. But he dares not face this thought! Moreover, since he is aware, however dimly, that his opinions are not rational, he becomes furious when they are disputed.

Maybe that's the reason why, for many centuries, you could be killed for doubting dogmas. Believers killing nonbelievers was a pattern long before the Ayatollah Khomeini ordered a holy hit on Salman Rushdie. For example:

In the fifth century BCE, the Greek teacher Protagoras wrote: "As to the gods, I have no way of knowing either that they exist or do not exist, or what they are like."

Protagoras was charged with impiety, as were other Greek thinkers. Unlike Socrates and Anaxagoras, who were sentenced to death, Protagoras merely was banished from Athens, and his books were burned. As he sailed into exile, he drowned.

In the year 415, the woman scientist Hypatia, head of the legendary Alexandria library, was beaten to death by Christian monks who considered her a pagan. The leader of the monks, Cyril, was canonized a saint.

In the eleventh century, Omar Khayyam wrote his exquisite Persian verses on the futility of trying to discern any purpose of life. He scoffed at believers yearning for heaven and belittled divine prophecies:

> The revelations of the devout and learn'd
> Who rose before us and as prophets burn'd
> Are all but stories, which, awoke from sleep
> They told their comrades, and to sleep return'd.

How did Omar escape execution in the Muslim world, which is known for beheading "blasphemers"? Actually, Omar is a mystery, and the verses attributed to him didn't begin surfacing until two centuries after his death.

In the 1500s, Michel de Montaigne, who created the essay as a literary form, wrote comments such as: "Man is certainly stark mad: he cannot make a worm, yet he will make gods by the dozen."

Although Montaigne lived at a time when "heretics" were burned, he eluded prosecution. Other thinkers weren't so lucky. In 1553, the physician Michael Servetus, who discovered the pulmonary circulation of blood, was burned alive in John Calvin's Geneva for doubting the Trinity. (In my Unitarian church, the youth group holds a yearly "Michael Servetus wiener roast" in his memory.)

In 1600, the philosopher Giordano Bruno was burned for

teaching that the earth circles the sun and that the universe is infinite. He was among thousands of Inquisition victims.

Later in the 1600s, the Englishman Thomas Hobbes, generally deemed the first major thinker in what is now called the Age of Reason, wrote: "Opinion of ghosts, ignorance of second causes, devotion to what men fear, and taking of things casual for prognostics, consisteth the natural seeds of religion."

A bishop accused Hobbes of atheism. Parliament ordered an investigation. Hobbes hastily burned his manuscripts and escaped with only a ban against future writings.

Baruch Spinoza, a Jew in Amsterdam, doubted theological dogmas and wrote lines such as: "Popular religion may be summed up as a respect for ecclesiastics." He was excommunicated by the Dutch synagogue and lived as a semi-outcast.

Gradually, the iron fist of religion lost its grip in the West, and disbelief became a bit safer. But there were relapses. For example, a French teenager was beheaded and burned in 1766 for marring a crucifix, singing irreverent songs, and wearing his hat while a church procession passed. Voltaire tried to save him, but the clergy demanded death, and the French parliament decreed it.

And Denis Diderot, creator of the first encyclopedia, was jailed for skepticism and his writings were burned. And English publishers who printed Thomas Paine's *The Age of Reason* were jailed for blasphemy.

Despite the risks, thinkers kept on questioning, and the right to doubt gradually was established—in the West, but not in the Muslim world, where "blasphemers" still face death today.

Although the right was won, it remains partly muzzled in America. What schoolchild is taught that Thomas Jefferson wrote many sneers at "priestcraft"—that he was denounced as a "howling atheist"—and that his famous vow of "eternal hostility against every form of tyranny over the mind of man," which is engraved in his memorial in Washington, was written of the clergy?

What student hears scientific explanations of religion, such as this one: Sigmund Freud said the widespread belief in a father-god arises from psychology. Each tiny child is awed by his or her father as a seemingly all-powerful protector and punisher. As maturity comes, the real father grows less awesome. But the infantile image remains hidden in the subconscious and becomes attached to an omnipotent, magical father in an invisible heaven. Unknowingly, Freud said, believers worship the long-forgotten toddler impression of the biological father, "clothed in the grandeur in which he once appeared to the small child."

Although open agnosticism is a no-no in America—and although fundamentalism is booming—supernatural religion is fading among educated people. America's mainline Protestant churches, formerly the domain of the elite, have lost millions of members since the 1960s. Intelligent people don't take miracles seriously and realize there's no evidence of a spirit realm.

The old church "thou shalt nots" against sex, liquor, gambling, birth control, dancing, Sunday shopping, and so on, have subsided in our lifetime. Fundamentalism may be rising, but so is secularism. Educated Americans are becoming like Europeans, who have mostly abandoned religion.

Soon it may be acceptable to challenge the supernatural, as so many great figures have done. The tacit code of silence—the last taboo—may be near an end. I certainly hope so.

NOTES

Sources of quotations, in sequence as they appear:

Thomas Jefferson—letter to John Adams, April 11, 1823.

Albert Einstein—*New York Times* commentary, November 9, 1930.

Mark Twain—*Mark Twain's Notebooks and Journals*, ed. Frederick Anderson, 1979, notebook 27, August 1887–July 1888.

Emily Brontë—*No Coward Soul*, January 1846.

Sigmund Freud—letter to Charles Singer.

Thomas Paine—*The Age of Reason*, 1794.

Thomas Edison—interview by Edward Marshall in the *New York Times*, October 2, 1910, front of Magazine Section.

Voltaire—letter to Frederick the Great, quoted in the *Encyclopedia of Unbelief* (Amherst, NY: Prometheus Books, 1985), p. 715.

Margaret Sanger—masthead of her newsletter, *The Woman Rebel*, quoted in the 1994 Women of Freethought Calendar, by Carole Gray, Columbus, Ohio.

Clarence Darrow—speech at Toronto, 1930, cited in *The Great Quotations*, by George Seldes (New York: Lyle Stuart, 1960), p. 190.

William Howard Taft—*The Life and Times of William Howard Taft*, by Harry F. Pringle (New York: Farrar & Rinehart, 1939), p. 373.

Luther Burbank—*San Francisco Bulletin*, January 22, 1926, p. 1, by Edgar Waite, headline: "I'm an Infidel, Declares Burbank, Casting Doubt on Soul Immortality Theory."

Bertrand Russell—opening lines of his 1930 essay "Has Religion Made Useful Contributions to Civilization?"

George Bernard Shaw—*Major Barbara*, preface, final paragraph.

Leo Tolstoy—letter dated April 4, 1901, to the Holy Synod of the Russian Orthodox Church, in response to his excommunication, cited in *Tolstoy*, by Henri Troyat (Garden City, NY: Doubleday, 1967), p. 591; and in *The Life of Lyof N. Tolstoi*, by Nathan Haskell Dole (New York: Scribner's, 1923), pp. 371–72.

Charles Darwin—"Life and Letters," cited in *Peter's Quotations*, by Laurance J. Peter (New York: Morrow, 1977), p. 45.

Kurt Vonnegut—*Peter's Quotations*, p. 191.

Gloria Steinem—*Peter's Quotations*, p. 103.

Russell, again—*Human Society in Ethics and Politics* (London: Allen & Unwin, 1954).

Protagoras—*On the Gods*.

Omar Khayyam—*The Rubaiyat of Omar Khayyam*, trans. Edward FitzGerald, 5th trans., 1889, verse 65; reprint Dover Thrift ed., 1990, p. 41.

Michel de Montaigne—"Apology to Raimond Sebond," *Essays*, 1580, bk. 2, chap. 12.

Thomas Hobbes—quoted by Rufus K. Noyes in *Views of Religion* (Boston: L. K. Washburn, 1906), p. 30.

Baruch Spinoza—quoted by Eugene Brussell in *The Dictionary of Quotable Definitions* (New York: Prentice-Hall, 1970), p. 490.

Jefferson, again—vow against tyranny, letter to Dr. Benjamin Rush, September 23, 1800.

Freud, again—father-god explanation from "The Future of an Illusion," in *The Freud Reader*, ed. Peter Gay (New York: Norton, 1989), pp. 694–96. Quote is from "New Introductory Lectures on Psychoanalysis," cited by Seldes in *The Great Quotations*, p. 261.

6

THE MEANING OF LIFE

Young seekers of truth go through a phase of wondering whether life has any discernible meaning. Why are we here? Why is the universe here? Is there a purpose to it all? This is the ultimate question, overarching all others.

The seekers usually plunge into philosophy and spend years sweating over "being" and "essence." And quibbling over how the mind obtains knowledge. And how we determine reality. And how language shapes our comprehension. In the end, most of them emerge (as I did) with no better answer than when they began—and a feeling that they wasted a lot of time and effort. Omar Khayyam felt the same way nine hundred years ago:

> Myself when young did eagerly frequent
> Doctor and saint, and heard great argument
>   About it and about, but evermore
> Came out by the same door as in I went.

Previously published in *Free Inquiry*, Winter 2001–2002.

However, despite this futility, I think intelligent people can address the meaning-of-life question sensibly, without bogging down in philosophical stewing and hair-splitting. That's what I'd like to do now: just spell out what's knowable as I see it. The following is my personal, amateur view.

First, 90 percent of humanity—the religious believers—needn't ask the meaning of life. Churches, mosques, and temples tell them the answer. Priests and scriptures say a magical, invisible god created the universe and put people here to be tested and set behavior rules for us to follow and created a heaven to reward the rule followers after they die and a hell to torture the rule-breakers and so on. This supernatural explanation, or some other mystical version, is accepted by the vast preponderance of the species.

But some of us can't swallow it because there's no evidence. Nobody can prove that people live after death. Nobody can prove that we are tortured or rewarded in an afterlife—or that there are invisible spirits to do the torturing and rewarding.

Therefore, we unsure people are doomed to be seekers, always searching for a meaning to life, but never quite finding one. I've been going through it for half a century. Now, I think I can declare that there are two clear answers: (1) Life has no meaning. (2) Life has a thousand meanings.

First, the lack of meaning: As for an ultimate purpose or transcending moral order, all the great thinkers since ancient Greece have failed to find one. The best philosophical minds have dug into this for twenty-five centuries without success. There have been endless theories, but no clear answer.

Martin Heidegger concluded that we are doomed to live our whole lives and die without knowing why we're here. That's existentialism: All we can really know is that we and the material world exist.

(Actually, I can know only one thing with absolute certainty: that my mind exists and is receiving impressions. Hypothetically, the images, sounds, feelings, and so forth, in my consciousness could be illusions—perhaps like artificial inputs to a brain in a laboratory tank—and the entire objective world could be fictitious. But there's no question whatsoever that my mind is receiving them. René Descartes stated this truth as *cogito, ergo sum*—I think, therefore I am. However, although we can't be totally sure of the validity of the sense impressions reaching our minds, we all presume that external people, places, and things actually exist. Their existence seems verified by thousands—millions—of encounters in our activities. We base our whole lives, and our search for knowledge, on this presumption that they are real.)

As we learn scientific facts, we realize that the universe is horribly violent, with stars exploding or disappearing into black holes. Here on Earth, nature can be equally monstrous. Both the cosmos and our biosphere seem utterly indifferent to humanity and care not a whit whether we live or die. Earthquakes and hurricanes and volcanos don't give a damn whether they hit us or miss us. Tigers, tapeworms, and bacteria consider us food.

As for morality, I don't think any exists, independent of people. It's merely rules that cultures evolve for themselves in their attempt to make life workable.

Conservatives talk of "natural law"—but there really is none. If Ku Klux Klansmen lynch a black from a limb, the tree doesn't care. Neither do the squirrels and birds in the branches. Neither does the sun or the moon above. Nature doesn't care. Only people care.

Take human rights. Thomas Jefferson said all people "are endowed by their Creator with certain unalienable rights." But I think Jefferson was wrong. There's no evidence that any Creator endowed anyone with any God-given rights. What unalienable rights were enjoyed by African blacks who were sold into slavery— including those on Jefferson's Monticello plantation?

What God-given rights were assured the three thousand victims of the historic terrorist attack on September 11, 2001? Or the six million Jews sent to Nazi death camps? Or the one million middle-class Cambodians murdered by Pol Pot's peasant army? Or the one million tall Tutsis killed by short Hutus? Or Ulster children killed by Catholic and Protestant bombs? Or Hiroshima residents in 1945? Or around one million women burned as witches by the Inquisition?

What's the meaning of life to the millions dying of AIDS? And the millions who died in the 1918 flu epidemic and in the Black Plague? And the nine hundred who gave cyanide to their children at Jonestown? Or the ninety who burned with their children in the David Koresh compound? What meaning existed for thousands of Hondurans drowned in hurricane floods a couple years ago? Or those sixteen Scottish kindergarten tots who were massacred by a psycho with pistols? Or the two thousand American women killed by their husbands or lovers every year? Or the twenty thousand victims the Aztecs sacrificed annually to the invisible flying serpent? Or the twenty thousand the Thugs strangled for the goddess Kali?

Meaningless, senseless, pointless—all these horrors have a grotesque absurdity about them. Words like *purpose, rights,* and *morals* simply don't apply.

I think these evils make it obvious, by simple logic, that there is no all-loving, all-merciful, all-compassionate, father-god. How could a kindly father watch idly while thousands of children die of leukemia, ignoring the desperate prayers of their families? Why would a kindly creator design nature so that lions slaughter antelopes, and pythons crush pigs, and sharks rip seals apart—and women die of breast cancer? Only a monster would arrange such monstrosities and do nothing to save the victims. Therefore, common sense proves that the beneficent modern god is a fantasy who doesn't exist.

In his book *Consilience,* the great Harvard sociobiologist E. O. Wilson pointed out that there are two fundamental ways of looking at reality: Empiricism, believing only what evidence tells you, and Transcendentalism, believing that a divine or cosmic moral order exists, independent of humanity. If any proof ever upholds the latter, he said, "the discovery would be quite simply the most consequential in human history."

So much for meaninglessness. Now for the many meanings.

Obviously, the reality of physics, chemistry, biology, atoms, cells, matter, radiation, and all the rest of nature imposes a physical order upon us. We can't escape the laws of nature that govern animals on an orbiting planet. And the inevitability of death is a force stronger than we are. We can't prevent it. Therefore, whatever meanings exist must apply to the temporary period while we live.

Clearly, there's a physical and psychological purpose to life. Our bodies need food, and clothing and shelter and health and affectionate comfort and security from violence and theft and so forth. We also need gregarious social reaction with people around us. And we need democratic freedoms, so we can speak honestly without fear of punishment—and justice, so we won't be treated cruelly.

These are the humanist purposes of life: to provide better nutrition, medicine, housing, transportation, education, safety, human rights, and all the other needs of people.

To attain this humanist "good life," the species has a strong need to raise intelligent, healthy, affectionate, responsible children. Sometimes I think the single biggest purpose in life is raising good kids.

I think we all endorse this biological/psychological meaning of life. We believe in preventing war, curing disease, ending hunger, improving literacy, reducing crime, averting famines, and taking other steps that make life pleasant—until death takes us.

However, aside from this "housekeeping" type of purpose, is there any greater meaning that transcends our human needs?

I don't think so. At least, I've never been able to find any proof of it. We simply must try to make life as good as possible and avoid horrors and care about people and have fun, even though we know that oblivion is coming.

Make hay while the sun shines—because darkness is on its way. Carpe diem—seize the day for now; live fully while you can. Omar Khayyam saw the folly of aggrandizing oneself because ill fortune or sickness and death soon wipe it out. And praying for heaven after death is even greater folly: "Fools, your reward is neither here nor there." So Omar's solution was to take comfort in verses, wine, and his lover "beside me singing in the wilderness—and wilderness is paradise enough." About fourteen hundred years before him, the great Greek skeptic Epicurus felt the same way.

So there you have it: We who are not orthodox religious believers can't find any underlying reason for existence. And we know that death looms ahead. So we must make the interval as enjoyable as possible, while we're here. This view of life's purpose was summed up a few years ago by the title of a Unitarian seminar: "Dancing over the Dark Abyss." And Zorba the Greek taught us: What is life, if not to dance?

7

JAMES BALDWIN

Here's an interesting literary footnote: The late James Baldwin, arguably America's greatest black writer, was a popular Pentecostal preacher in Harlem at age fourteen—but at seventeen he renounced religion as a sham.

Years later, he described his boyhood transformation in an essay titled "Down at the Cross," first published in the *New Yorker*, then reprinted in his civil rights book, *The Fire Next Time*.

He told of growing up amid the bitter hopelessness of the black ghetto, watching jobless men drink and fight, resenting tyrannical treatment by his preacher stepfather, wishing for escape. The misery around him "helped to hurl me into the church," he wrote.

One night at a prayer meeting, "everything came roaring, screaming, crying out, and I fell to the ground before the altar. It was the strangest sensation I have ever had in my life." He soon became a junior minister at the Fireside Pentecostal Assembly and became "a much bigger drawing card than my father."

Previously published in *Free Inquiry*, Fall 2000.

"That was the most frightening time of my life, and quite the most dishonest, and the resulting hysteria lent great passion to my sermons—for a while," he said. Considering all the evils of Harlem street life, "it was my good luck—perhaps—that I found myself in the church racket instead of some other and surrendered to a spiritual seduction long before I came to any carnal knowledge."

The "fire and excitement" of Pentecostalism were captivating, Baldwin wrote—but he sensed subconsciously that it was bogus, and by seventeen he suffered "the slow crumbling of my faith." It happened "when I began to read again. . . . I began, fatally, with Dostoevski."

He continued handing out gospel tracts but knew they were "impossible to believe. I was forced, reluctantly, to realize that the Bible itself had been written by men." As for the claim that the Bible writers were divinely inspired, he said he "knew by now, alas, far more about divine inspiration than I dared admit, for I knew how I worked myself up into my own visions."

Baldwin wrote that he might have remained in the church if "there was any loving-kindness to be found in the haven I represented." But he finally concluded that "there was no love in the church. It was a mask for hatred and self-hatred and despair." So his religion ended.

Years later, he visited Black Muslim leader Elijah Muhammad and concluded that Elijah's "revelations" about Satan creating "white devils" were just as irrational as Christian beliefs. When Elijah asked his faith, Baldwin replied: "I left the church twenty years ago, and I haven't joined anything since."

"And what are you now?" Elijah asked.

"I? Now? Nothing," the great writer replied.

Baldwin's superb humanism was summed up eloquently in this paragraph from "Down at the Cross":

Life is tragic simply because the earth turns and the sun inexorably rises and sets, and one day, for each of us, the sun will go down for the last, last time. Perhaps the whole root of our trouble, the human trouble, is that we will sacrifice all the beauty of our lives, will imprison ourselves in totems, taboos, crosses, blood sacrifices, steeples, mosques, races, armies, flags, nations, in order to deny the fact of death, which is the only fact we have.

8

SEX AND GOD: IS RELIGION TWISTED?

C hristian endeavor," H. L. Mencken wrote, "is notoriously hard on female pulchritude."

He was right, of course, and he should have included Jewish endeavor and Muslim endeavor in his observation. Western religions have spent millennia inflicting shame, guilt, repression, and punishment upon human sexuality—especially upon women's sexuality.

Asian faiths aren't so punitive. They generally accept lovemaking as a natural part of life. Some Hindu temples are covered with statues of copulating gods and goddesses. Millions of Shiva worshipers pray over models of his erect penis. Tantric sects practice ritual intercourse.

But the West presents an opposite, ugly story: a long chronicle of religious hostility to lovers—for no rational reason.

The Old Testament raged against "whoredom" and decreed brutal penalties for unapproved sex. It commanded that nonvirgin brides be stoned to death (Deut. 22:21).

Previously published in *Free Inquiry*, Fall 1997.

In the first century CE, Paul urged celibacy for Christians. The earliest known papal decree, issued by Pope Siricius in 386, attempted (without much success) to forbid church elders to make love with their wives. Scholar Reay Tannahill says early Christian leaders made sex and "sin" synonymous.

"It was Augustine who epitomized a general feeling among the church fathers that the act of intercourse was fundamentally disgusting," she wrote. "Arnobius called it filthy and degrading, Methodius unseemly, Jerome unclean, Tertullian shameful, Ambrose a defilement."[1]

Christian father Origen of Alexandria reportedly castrated himself in a traumatic display of faith.

When priests oversaw the historic witch hunts—in which thousands of women were tortured and burned—church writings reeked of revulsion to female sexuality. A medieval cardinal, Hughes de St. Cher, wrote: "Woman pollutes the body, drains the resources, kills the soul, uproots the strength, blinds the eye, and embitters the voice."[2]

When Puritans ruled England in the 1600s, death was decreed for adultery.

In late nineteenth-century America, Anthony Comstock and his "Committee for the Suppression of Vice" pursued sex like a hunted animal. About twenty-five hundred people were convicted on morality charges, and Congress passed the puritanical Comstock Laws. Margaret Sanger was jailed eight times for advocating birth control. Comstock even led a police raid against an art gallery that dared to display the naively innocent *September Morn* painting.

Until recently, thanks to church pressure, nearly every US state had Old Testament–style laws against "fornication" and "sodomy" and the like. It wasn't until 1972 that the US Supreme Court finally ruled that all American couples have a right to birth control. The clergy's opposition to contraception is based not so much on a desire for limitless breeding as a desire to prevent people from enjoying the sexual freedom brought by birth control.

Today, the church's ability to imprison nonconformists has receded. However, every censorship effort, every attempt at sexual repression, still comes from religion.

North Carolina's 1.2 million Southern Baptists once voted to shut off their television sets for a day to protest "moral depravity" in shows such as *NYPD Blue* containing partial nudity and sex.

Former Pope John Paul II declared unmarried sex and birth control "intrinsically evil." In Charleston, West Virginia, two brave nuns, Patricia Hussey and Barbara Ferraro, battled Catholicism's sexual taboos until they finally were forced out of their order. They recounted their struggle in a book, *No Turning Back*: "The church really hates the idea of people having sex for fun. . . . There is something prurient and dishonest about the church's loathing for the body."[3]

Sometimes the ministers who rail loudest against "filth" and "pornography" are cloaking their secret sins. Television evangelists Jimmy Swaggart and Jim Bakker both fell to private sex scandals. Numerous such cases appear in the news.

As American clergy endlessly strive to censor sex from public media, an odd contradiction has arisen: Ministers raise little objection to a movie containing fifty murders—but a glimpse of a woman's nipple brings their wrath. A popular song, "The Windmills of Your Mind," commented: "Bullets fly like popcorn on the screen, recommended wholesome, nice, and clean. Making love's the thing that can't be seen. Why?"

(Using legal language, Congress and state legislatures periodically ponder laws to imprison purveyors of "ultimate sexual acts." In my newspaper, I once asked readers to suggest what might be an ultimate sexual act. Lovers in a rubber raft going over Niagara Falls? Two elephants in a china shop?)

Meanwhile, the sexual hang-ups of Christianity today are trivial compared with those in the Muslim world, where suppression of women continues at Old Testament levels. Some examples:

- In Muslim Somalia, an estimated 98 percent of girls are genitally mutilated to inhibit their sexual pleasure throughout their lives and to keep them "pure" for husbands. But it doesn't always work. In 1993, a United Nations team found five women being stoned to death for adultery. They had been condemned by mosque leaders, and the execution was carried out after evening prayers. Cheering villagers videotaped the killing. UN observers who tried to save the women were driven off by threats of death. UN agent Cecelia Kamau said bitterly: "Fundamentalism is really catching on."

- In Muslim Algeria, zealots shoot high school girls in the face for not wearing veils and cut the throats of professors who teach boys and girls in the same classrooms.

- In Muslim Iran, morality patrols flog women who allow a lock of hair to show beneath their shrouds, and clerics laboriously black out women's faces in imported magazines.

- In Muslim Saudi Arabia, a teenage princess and her lover were executed in public in 1977 for the crime of making love.

- In Muslim Afghanistan, a major *mujahideen* (holy warrior) leader—one of those praised by President Ronald Reagan as "freedom fighters"—got his start by throwing acid in the faces of unveiled college girls. After the even-more-puritanical Taliban religious students seized Afghanistan, they decreed that all windows must be painted black, lest someone look at a woman through one, and they stoned women to death for being in the company of an unrelated man.

It would probably take an army of psychiatrists and historians to pinpoint all the reasons why Western religion developed such antagonism toward human sexuality. More important is the question: Is this attitude justified? Are there ethical, rational reasons to support the religious condemnations of normal human desires?

Perhaps the most detailed and insightful answer came from none other than humanist Bertrand Russell, who said a "morbid and unnatural" attitude toward sex is "the worst feature of the Christian religion." And much of what he said applies with equal force to the other Western religions. He asserted that the church's aversion to sex is not only unfounded but also harmful. Against the prevailing antisex views of religion, he argued that sexual pleasure is a positive good and that religious objections are based not on reason but on dogma. But perhaps his most important argument was that religious antisexuality attitudes inflict untold human misery, especially on women. He observed: "Monks have always regarded Woman primarily as the temptress. They have thought of her mainly as the inspirer of impure lusts." So the church has done "what it could to secure that the only form of sex which it permitted should involve very little pleasure and great deal of pain. The opposition to birth control has, in fact, the same motive."[4]

Strangely, Russell observed, the church doesn't seem to care how miserable its rigid sex laws make people. He cited this example:

> An inexperienced girl is married to a syphilitic man; in that case the Catholic Church says, "This is an indissoluble sacrament. You must endure celibacy or stay together. And if you stay together, you must not use birth control to prevent the birth of syphilitic children." Nobody whose natural sympathies have not been warped by dogma, or whose moral nature was not absolutely dead to all sense of suffering, could maintain that it is right and proper that that state of things should continue. . . .
>
> The church, by its insistence upon what it chooses to call morality, inflicts upon all sorts of people undeserved and unnecessary suffering . . . because it has chosen to label as morality a certain narrow set of rules of conduct which have nothing to do with human happiness; and when you say that this or that ought to be done because it would make for human happiness, they think that has nothing to do with the matter at all. "What has human happiness to do with morals? The object of morals is not to make people happy."[5]

In other words, people are less important to the church than the harsh rules it adopted centuries ago. Scholar Gerald Larue, author of *Sex and the Bible*, says: "When biblical sexual taboos serve to produce guilt and deny normal and natural sexual behavior, their influence is toxic."[6]

Ironically, century after century of holy hostility to sex hasn't dampened humanity's zest for it. A 1992 World Health Organization report estimated that more than 100 million couples around the globe make love in a single day. And people relish sexual entertainment as well. A recent issue of *U.S. News & World Report* was devoted to the astounding rise of the sex business in America:

Last year Americans spent more than $8 billion on hard-core videos, live sex acts, adult cable programming, sexual devices, computer porn and sex magazines—an amount much larger than Hollywood's domestic box office receipts and larger than all the revenues generated by rock and country music albums. Americans now spend more money at strip clubs than at Broadway, Off-Broadway, regional and nonprofit theaters, at the opera, the ballet, and jazz and classical music performances—combined.[7]

If Americans rent 665 million X-rated videos each year, as the report said, while conservative churches still say sex is "filth" or "intrinsically evil," someone is out of step with reality. And it isn't the billions of people who know, deep in their psyches, that lovemaking is intrinsically good.

Most Westerners have come to regard sex as wholesome and wonderful. Sanctimonious strictures suit fewer and fewer people. Episcopal priest Raymond Lawrence wrote in a national United Methodist journal: "The churches are in danger of evolving into havens for the sexually suppressed or, worse, communities of profound hypocrisy."[8]

True—but the record of the centuries shows clearly that Western religion has always been a haven for the sexually suppressed.

NOTES

1. Reay Tannahill, *Sex in History* (New York: Stein & Day, 1980), p. 141.

2. Wayland Young, *Eros Denied: Sex in Western Society* (New York: Grove Press, 1964), p. 201.

3. Barbara Ferraro, Patricia Hussey, and Jane O'Reilly, *No Turning Back: Two Nuns' Battle with the Vatican over Women's Right to Choose* (New York: Poseidon Press, 1990).

4. Bertrand Russell, "Has Religion Made Useful Contributions to Civilization?" (1930), reprinted in *Why I Am Not a Christian and Other Essays on Religion and Related Subjects* (New York: Simon & Schuster, 1957), p. 27.

5. Bertrand Russell, "Why I Am Not a Christian," lecture on March 6, 1927, to National Secular Society South London branch at Battersea Town Hall, reprinted as a pamphlet, and later included in *Why I Am Not a Christian and Other Essays on Religion and Related Subjects*, pp. 21–22.

6. Gerald Larue, interview, *USA Today* magazine, September 1985.

7. Eric Schlosser, "The Business of Pornography," *U.S. News & World Report*, February 10, 1997, p. 44.

8. Raymond J. Lawrence, "The Church and the Sexual Revolution," *Quarterly Review* (Spring 1985), excerpted by Words by Wire and reprinted in the *Milwaukee Journal*, July 14, 1985, p. 23.

9

WHERE DO BELIEFS COME FROM?

Suppose a miracle is reported—say, another Virgin Mary sighting by Catholics, or the nine-hundred-foot Jesus seen by evangelist Oral Roberts. Some Americans will embrace this news joyfully, as evidence of the holy, while others will be skeptical.

Here's my question: What causes some people to believe such reports and others to doubt them? What is different inside the minds of the two groups? What makes believers and doubters?

I really don't know—and neither do any of the believers or doubters, I suspect.

This quandary applies to more than religion. It covers all human belief systems. For example, what causes some people to be political conservatives and others liberals—right wingers and left wingers? What creates rebels and conformists, puritans and playboys, social reformers and traditionalists, militarists and pacifists ("hawks" and "doves"), Democrats and Republicans, gun lovers and gun haters, environmen-

Previously published in the *Charleston Gazette*, May 4, 2003, and syndicated nationally.

talists and industry boosters ("tree huggers" and "spoilers"), death-penalty advocates and death-penalty foes, and so on?

A half century ago, why did some Americans support racial segregation and some integration? A century earlier, why did some clergymen uphold slavery and others denounce it?

Nearly everyone has a "worldview" encompassing such issues—but does anyone know how he or she acquired it? Where do beliefs come from? Over the years, I've put this question to various psychologists, but I never got an answer I can understand.

If you ask, say, a conservative why he's conservative, you'll probably get an answer something like: "Because I'm intelligent and can see the obvious correctness of that position." And a liberal would say exactly the same. Neither really knows why.

Odd "agendas" of beliefs exist. Protestant fundamentalists usually want to censor sexy movies, ban abortion, impose the death penalty, punish gays, allow pistol carrying, ban marijuana, curtail sex education, reduce welfare, outlaw go-go girls, and require prayer in schools. But why is there a link between sexual taboos, executions, and welfare? Offhand, the topics don't seem related.

Conversely, secular liberals generally back an opposite agenda on all those subjects. And Catholics often are switch hitters, opposing sex while embracing share-the-wealth efforts. How are these outlooks implanted?

In psychology, there's a factor called "bias reinforcement." It means that people with certain inclinations constantly look for evidence to back their views and shrug off opposing evidence. Does that help explain beliefs? Do we condition ourselves, like Pavlov's dog, to give knee-jerk reactions to stimuli? Some new research implies that beliefs may be partly genetic, locked into our DNA.

More than a century ago, in a lecture titled "The Will to Believe," famed philosopher/novelist/psychologist William James told Ivy League students that people believe what they want to believe—what their personal orientations draw them to accept—and that this human instinct is desirable. This is called "volitionalism" by scholars. But it really doesn't explain anything. For example, it doesn't clarify why evangelist Jerry Falwell is drawn to believe the word-for-word truth of the Bible but renowned astronomer Carl Sagan was drawn to reject it.

In some cases, circumstantial causes of beliefs are visible. For example, women traditionally held nurturing roles, while men went forth to conquer. So women tend to be "liberal," supporting school lunches, healthcare, welfare, and so forth, while men are inclined to militarism. (Women are from Venus, men from Mars.) Blacks have been cheated in America for so long that they naturally see society from an underdog view—rallying behind O. J. Simpson, for instance. Underdog feelings apply even stronger to gays. Most Jews feel an ethnic affinity for Israel and can't be objective about Mideast politics. Ditto, in reverse, for Arabs.

Growing up in a working-class family or in poverty—instead of being born to wealth and privilege—undoubtedly inclines many to embrace labor-union beliefs and egalitarian causes. But there are exceptions to all these patterns. And other belief roots are too unfathomable for such simplistic explanations.

Beliefs of the whole society evolve. When I was young in the 1950s, gays were put in prison, and it also was a crime to buy a drink, look at a "girlie" magazine, buy a lottery ticket, marry someone of a different race, or have sex out of wedlock. Today, the beliefs behind those laws seem as antiquated as powdered wigs.

In the end, I'm still mostly unable to deduce why people are religious believers or skeptics, political conservatives or liberals, moral puritans or fun seekers, military hawks or doves, and all the rest. Yet these are powerful psychological forces that shape the very nature of our society and its internal conflicts. Where do beliefs come from? It is a puzzlement.

10

HOLY HORRORS

A pig caused hundreds of Indians to kill one another in 1980. The animal walked through a Muslim holy ground at Moradabad, near New Delhi. Muslims, who think pigs are an embodiment of Satan, blamed Hindus for the defilement. They went on a murder rampage, stabbing and clubbing Hindus, who retaliated in kind. The pig riot spread to a dozen cities and left more than two hundred dead.

This swinish episode tells a universal tale. It typifies religious behavior that has been recurring for centuries.

Ronald Reagan often called religion the world's mightiest force for good, "the bedrock of moral order." George Bush said it gives people "the character they need to get through life." This view is held by millions. But the truism isn't true. The record of human experience shows that where religion is strong, it causes cruelty. Intense beliefs produce intense hostility. Only when faith loses its force can a society hope to become humane.

Previously published in *Penthouse*, August 1990.

The history of religion is a horror story. If anyone doubts it, just review this chronicle of religion's gore during the last thousand years or so:

- The First Crusade was launched in 1095 with the battle cry "Deus Vult" (God wills it), a mandate to destroy infidels in the Holy Land. Gathering crusaders in Germany first fell upon "the infidel among us," Jews in the Rhine valley, thousands of whom were dragged from their homes or hiding places and hacked to death or burned alive. Then the religious legions plundered their way two thousand miles to Jerusalem, where they killed virtually every inhabitant, "purifying" the symbolic city. Cleric Raymond of Aguilers wrote: "In the temple of Solomon, one rode in blood up to the knees and even to the horses' bridles, by the just and marvelous judgment of God."

- The Mayan theocracy, which flourished between the eleventh and sixteenth centuries, was the first Central American culture to practice human sacrifice. To appease various gods, maidens were drowned in sacred wells and other victims had their hearts cut out, were shot with arrows, or were beheaded. Elsewhere, sacrifice was sporadic. In Peru, pre-Inca tribes killed children in temples called "houses of the moon." In Tibet, Bon shamans performed ritual killings. In Borneo, builders of pile houses drove the first pile through the body of a maiden to pacify the earth goddess. In India, Dravidian people offered lives to village goddesses, and followers of Kali sacrificed a male child every Friday evening.

- In the Third Crusade, after Richard the Lion-Hearted captured Acre in 1191, he ordered three thousand captives—many of them women and children—to be taken outside the city and slaughtered. Some were disemboweled in a search for swallowed gems. Bishops intoned blessings. Infidel lives were of no consequence. As Saint Bernard of Clairvaux declared in launching the Second Crusade: "The Christian glories in the death of a pagan, because thereby Christ himself is glorified."

- The Assassins were a sect of Ismaili Shi'ite Muslims whose faith required the stealthy murder of religious opponents. From the eleventh to the thirteenth centuries, they killed numerous leaders in modern-day Iran, Iraq, and Syria. They finally were wiped out by conquering Mongols—but their vile name survives.

- Throughout Europe, beginning in the 1100s, tales spread that Jews were abducting Christian children, sacrificing them, and using their blood in rituals. Hundreds of massacres stemmed from this "blood libel." Some of the supposed sacrifice victims—Little Saint Hugh of Lincoln, the holy child of LaGuardia, Simon of Trent—were beatified or commemorated with shrines that became sites of pilgrimages and miracles.

- In 1209, Pope Innocent III launched an armed crusade against Albigenses Christians in southern France. When the besieged city of Beziers fell, soldiers reportedly asked their papal adviser how to distinguish the faithful from the infidel among the captives. He commanded: "Kill them all. God will know his own." Nearly twenty thousand were slaughtered—many first blinded, mutilated, dragged behind horses, or used for target practice.

- The Fourth Lateran Council in 1215 proclaimed the doctrine of transubstantiation: that the host wafer miraculously turns into the body of Jesus during the mass. Soon rumors spread that Jews were stealing the sacred wafers and stabbing or driving nails through them to crucify Jesus again. Reports said that the pierced host bled, cried out, or emitted spirits. On this charge, Jews were burned at the stake in 1243 in Belitz, Germany—the first of many killings that continued into the 1800s. To avenge the tortured host, the German knight Rindfliesch led a brigade in 1298 that exterminated 146 defenseless Jewish communities in six months.

- In the 1200s, the Incas built their empire in Peru, a society dominated by priests reading daily magical signs and offering sacrifices to appease many gods. At major ceremonies, up to two hundred children were burned as offerings. Special "chosen women"—comely virgins without blemish—were strangled.

- Also during the 1200s, the hunt for Albigensian heretics led to establishment of the Inquisition, which spread over Europe. Pope Innocent IV authorized torture. Under interrogation by Dominican priests, screaming victims were stretched, burned, pierced, and broken on fiendish pain machines to make them confess to disbelief and to identify fellow transgressors. Inquisitor Robert le Bourge sent 183 people to the stake in a single week.

- In Spain, where many Jews and Moors had converted to escape persecution, inquisitors sought those harboring their old faith. At least two thousand Spanish backsliders were burned. Executions in other countries included the burning of scientists such as mathematician-philosopher Giordano Bruno, who espoused Copernicus's theory that the planets orbit the sun.

- When the Black Death swept Europe in 1348–1349, rumors alleged that it was caused by Jews poisoning wells. Hysterical mobs slaughtered thousands of Jews in several countries. In Speyer, Germany, the burned bodies were piled into giant wine casks and sent floating down the Rhine. In northern Germany, Jews were walled up alive in their homes to suffocate or starve. The Flagellants, an army of penitents who whipped themselves bloody, stormed the Jewish quarter of Frankfurt in a gruesome massacre. The prince of Thuringia announced that he had burned his Jews for the honor of God.

- The Aztecs began their elaborate theocracy in the 1300s and brought human sacrifice to a golden era. About twenty thousand people were killed yearly to appease gods—especially the sun god, who needed daily "nourishment" of blood. Hearts of sacrifice victims were cut out, and some bodies were eaten ceremoniously. Other victims were drowned, beheaded, burned, or dropped from heights. In a rite to the rain god, shrieking children were killed at several sites so that their tears might induce rain. In a rite to the maize goddess, a virgin danced for twenty-four hours, then was killed and skinned; her skin was worn by a priest in further dancing. One account says that at King Ahuitzotl's coronation, eighty thousand prisoners were butchered to please the gods.

- In the 1400s, the Inquisition shifted its focus to witchcraft. Priests tortured untold thousands of women into confessing that they were witches who flew through the sky and engaged in sex with the devil—then they were burned or hanged for their confessions. Witch hysteria raged for three centuries in a dozen nations. Estimates of the number executed vary from a hundred thousand to two million. Whole villages were exterminated. In the first half of the seventeenth century, about five thousand "witches" were put to death in the French province of Alsace, and nine hundred were burned in the Bavarian city of Bamberg. The witch craze was religious madness at its worst.

- The "Protestant Inquisition" is a term applied to the severities of John Calvin in Geneva and Queen Elizabeth I in England during the 1500s. Calvin's followers burned fifty-eight "heretics," including theologian Michael Servetus, who doubted the Trinity. Elizabeth I outlawed Catholicism and executed about two hundred Catholics.

- Protestant Huguenots grew into an aggressive minority in France in the 1500s—until repeated Catholic reprisals smashed them. On Saint Bartholomew's Day in 1572, Catherine de Medicis secretly authorized Catholic dukes to send their soldiers into Huguenot quarters and slaughter families. This massacre touched off a six-week bloodbath in which Catholics murdered about ten thousand Huguenots. Other persecutions continued for two centuries, until the French Revolution. One group of Huguenots escaped to Florida; in 1565 a Spanish brigade discovered their colony, denounced their heresy, and killed them all.

- Members of India's Thuggee sect strangled people as sacrifices to appease the bloodthirsty goddess Kali, a practice beginning in the 1500s. The number of victims has been estimated to be as high as two million. Thugs were claiming about twenty thousand lives a year in the 1800s until British rulers stamped them out. At a trial in 1840, one Thug was accused of killing 931 people. Today, some Hindu priests still sacrifice goats to Kali.

- The Anabaptists, communal "rebaptizers," were slaughtered by both Catholic and Protestant authorities. In Munster, Germany, Anabaptists took control of the city, drove out the clergymen, and proclaimed a New Zion. The bishop of Munster began an armed siege. While the townspeople starved, the Anabaptist leader proclaimed himself king and executed dissenters. When Munster finally fell, the chief Anabaptists were tortured to death with red-hot pincers and their bodies hung in iron cages from a church steeple.

- Oliver Cromwell was deemed a moderate because he massacred only Catholics and Anglicans, not other Protestants. This Puritan general commanded Bible-carrying soldiers, whom he roused to religious fervor. After decimating an Anglican army, Cromwell said, "God made them as stubble to our swords." He demanded the beheading of the defeated King Charles I and made himself the holy dictator of England during the 1650s. When his army crushed the hated Irish Catholics, he ordered the execution of the surrendered defenders of Drogheda and their priests, calling it "a righteous judgment of God upon these barbarous wretches."

- Ukrainian Bogdan Chmielnicki was a Cossack Cromwell. He wore the banner of Eastern Orthodoxy in a holy war against Jews and Polish Catholics. More than a hundred thousand were killed in this seventeenth-century bloodbath, and the Ukraine was split away from Poland to become part of the Orthodox Russian Empire.

- The Thirty Years' War produced the largest religious death toll in Europe. It began in 1618 when Protestant leaders threw two Catholic emissaries out of a Prague window into a dung heap. War flared between Catholic and Protestant princedoms, drawing in supportive religious armies from Germany, Spain, England, Holland, Denmark, Sweden, France, and Italy. Sweden's Protestant soldiers sang Martin Luther's "Ein' Feste Burg" in battle. Three decades of combat turned central Europe into a wasteland of misery. One estimate states that Germany's population dropped from eighteen million to four million. In the end nothing was settled, and too few people remained to rebuild cities, plant fields, or conduct education.

- When Puritans settled in Massachusetts in the 1600s, they created a religious police state where doctrinal deviation could lead to flogging, pillorying, hanging, cutting off ears, or boring through the tongue with a hot iron. Preaching Quaker beliefs was a capital offense. Four stubborn Quakers defied this law and were hanged. In the 1690s, fear of witches seized the colony. Twenty alleged witches were killed and 150 others imprisoned.

- In 1723, the bishop of Gdansk, Poland, demanded that all Jews be expelled from the city. The town council declined, but the bishop's exhortations roused a mob that invaded the ghetto and beat the residents to death.

- Islamic jihads (holy wars), mandated by the Koran, killed millions over twelve centuries. In early years, Muslim armies spread the faith rapidly: east to India and west to Morocco. Then splintering sects branded other Muslims as infidels and declared jihads against them. The Kharijis battled Sunni rulers. The Azariqis decreed death to all "sinners" and their families. In 1804, a Sudanese holy man, Usman dan Fodio, waged a bloody jihad that broke the religious sway of the Sultan of Gobir. In the 1850s, another Sudanese mystic, El Hadj Umar Tall, led a barbaric jihad to convert pagan African tribes—with massacres, beheadings, and a mass execution of three hundred hostages. In the 1880s, a third Sudanese holy man, Muhammad Ahmed, commanded a jihad that destroyed a ten-thousand-man Egyptian army and wiped out defenders of Khartoum led by British general Charles "Chinese" Gordon.

- In 1801, Orthodox priests in Bucharest, Romania, revived the story that Jews sacrificed Christians and drank their blood. Enraged parishioners stormed the ghetto and cut the throats of 128 Jews.

- When the Baha'i faith began in Persia in 1844, the Islamic regime sought to exterminate it. The Baha'i founder was imprisoned and executed in 1850. Two years later, the religious government massacred twenty thousand Baha'is. Streets of Tehran were soaked with blood. The new Baha'i leader, Baha'ullah, was tortured and exiled in foreign Muslim prisons for the rest of his life.

- Human sacrifices were still occurring in Buddhist Burma in the 1850s. When the capital was moved to Mandalay, fifty-six "spotless" men were buried beneath the new city walls to sanctify and protect the city. When two of the burial spots were later found empty, royal astrologers decreed that five hundred men, women, boys, and girls must be killed and buried at once, or the capital must be abandoned. About a hundred were actually buried before British governors stopped the ceremonies.

- In 1857, both Muslim and Hindu taboos triggered the Sepoy Mutiny in India. British rulers had given their native soldiers new paper cartridges that had to be bitten open. The cartridges were greased with animal tallow. This enraged Muslims, to whom pigs are unclean, and Hindus, to whom cows are sacred. Troops of both faiths went into a crazed mutiny, killing Europeans wantonly. At Kanpur, hundreds of European women and children were massacred after being promised safe passage.

- Late in the nineteenth century, with rebellion stirring in Russia, the czar's police attempted to divert public attention by helping anti-Semitic groups rouse Orthodox Christian hatred for Jews. Three waves of pogroms ensued—in the 1880s, from 1903 to 1906, and during the Russian Revolution. Each wave was increasingly murderous. During the final period, 530 communities were attacked and sixty thousand Jews were killed.

- In the early 1900s, Muslim Turks waged genocide against Christian Armenians, and Christian Greeks and Balkans warred against the Islamic Ottoman Empire.

- When India finally won independence from Britain in 1947, the "great soul" of Mahatma Gandhi wasn't able to prevent Hindus and Muslims from turning on one another in a killing frenzy that took perhaps one million lives. Even Gandhi was killed by a Hindu who thought him too pro-Muslim.

- Starting in the 1950s, recurring combat between Christians, animists, and Muslims in Sudan killed an estimated two million.

- In Jonestown, Guyana, in 1978, followers of the Rev. Jim Jones killed a visiting congressman and three newsmen, then administered cyanide to themselves and their children in a nine-hundred-person suicide that shocked the world.

- Islamic religious law decrees that thieves shall have their hands or feet chopped off, and unmarried lovers shall be killed. In the Sudan in 1983 and 1984, sixty-six thieves were axed in public. A moderate Muslim leader, Mahmoud Mohammed Taha, was hanged for heresy in 1985 because he opposed these amputations. In Saudi Arabia a teenage princess and her lover were executed in public in 1977. In Pakistan in 1987, a twenty-five-year-old carpenter's daughter was sentenced to be stoned to death for engaging in unmarried sex. In the United Arab Emirates in 1984, a cook and a maid were sentenced to stoning for adultery—but, as a show of mercy, the execution was postponed until after the maid's baby was born.

- In Darkley, Northern Ireland, in 1983, Catholic terrorists with automatic weapons burst into a Protestant church on a Sunday morning and opened fire, killing three worshipers and wounding seven. It was just one of hundreds of Catholic-Protestant ambushes that took nearly three thousand lives in Ulster after age-old religious hostility turned violent again in 1969.

- Hindu-Muslim bloodshed erupts randomly throughout India. More than three thousand were killed in Assam province in 1983. Not long afterward, Muslims hung dirty sandals on a Hindu leader's portrait as a religious insult. This act triggered a week of arson riots that left 216 dead, 756 wounded, 13,000 homeless, and 4,100 in jail. Hundreds of similar sectarian clashes have occurred since.

- Religious tribalism—segregation of sects into hostile camps— ravaged Lebanon in the 1980s. News reports of the civil war told of "Maronite Christian snipers," "Sunni Muslim suicide bombers," "Druze machine gunners," "Shi'ite Muslim mortar fire," and "Alawite Muslim shootings." Some 130,000 people died and a once-lovely nation was ravaged.

- In Nigeria in 1982, religious fanatic followers of Mallam Marwa killed and mutilated several hundred people as heretics and infidels. They drank the blood of some of the victims. When the militia arrived to quell the violence, the cultists sprinkled themselves with blessed powder that they thought would make them impervious to police bullets. It didn't.

- The Shi'ite theocracy in Iran—"the government of God on earth"—decreed that Baha'i believers who won't convert shall be killed. About two hundred stubborn Baha'is were executed in the early 1980s, including women and teenagers. Up to forty thousand Baha'is fled the country. Sex taboos in Iran are so severe that (1) any woman who shows a lock of hair is jailed; (2) Western magazines being shipped into the country first go to censors who laboriously black out all women's photos except for faces; (3) women aren't allowed to ski with men but have a separate slope where they may ski in shrouds.

- The lovely island nation of Sri Lanka has been turned hellish by ambushes and massacres between Buddhist Sinhalese and Hindu Tamils.

- In 1983, a revered Muslim leader, Mufti Sheikh Sa'ad e-Din el'Alami of Jerusalem, issued a fatwa (an order of divine deliverance) promising an eternal place in paradise to any Muslim assassin who would kill President Hafiz al-Assad of Syria.

- Sikhs want to create a separate theocracy, Khalistan (Land of the Pure), in the Punjab region of India. Many heeded the late extremist preacher Jarnail Bhindranwale, who taught his followers that they have a "religious duty to send opponents to hell." Throughout the 1980s, they sporadically murdered Hindus to accomplish this goal. In 1984, after Sikh guards riddled prime minister Indira Gandhi with fifty bullets, Hindus went on a rampage that killed five thousand Sikhs in three days. Mobs dragged Sikhs from homes, stores, buses, and trains, chopping and pounding them to death. Some were burned alive; boys were castrated.

- In 1984, Shi'ite fanatics who killed and tortured Americans on a hijacked Kuwaiti airliner at Tehran Airport said they did it "for the pleasure of God."

Obviously, people who think religion is a force for good are looking only at Dr. Jekyll and ignoring Mr. Hyde. They don't see the superstitious savagery pervading both history and current events.

During the past three centuries, religion gradually lost its power over life in Europe and America, and church horrors ended in the West. But the poison lingered. The Nazi Holocaust was rooted in centuries of religious hate. Historian Dagobert Runes said the long era of church persecution killed three and a half million Jews—and Hitler's Final Solution was a secular continuation. Meanwhile, faith remains potent in the third world, where it still produces familiar results.

It's fashionable among thinking people to say that religion isn't the real cause of today's strife in Lebanon, Sri Lanka, Northern Ireland, India, and Iran—that sects merely provide labels for combatants. Not so. Religion keeps the groups in hostile camps. Without it, divisions would blur with passing generations; children would adapt to new times, mingle, intermarry, forget ancient wounds. But religion keeps them alien to one another.

Anything that divides people breeds inhumanity. Religion serves that ugly purpose.

11

NIKOS KAZANTZAKIS

I n 1988, fundamentalist Christians in several nations vented rage
and violence because a movie, *The Last Temptation of Christ*, portrayed Jesus as a wavering human, lusting for the prostitute Mary
Magdalene.

A Parisian theater showing the film was firebombed, sending
thirteen people to hospitals. Another at Besancon, France, suffered a
similar attack. Tear gas was loosed in some French movie houses.
Israel's government banned the film. In America, theaters were ran-
sacked, one was burned, another had its screen slashed, and a
screaming protester crashed a bus into a theater lobby. About
twenty-five thousand evangelicals picketed Universal Studios in
Hollywood, and smaller throngs protested in several cities. Catholic
bishops and TV evangelists denounced the movie angrily. Some filed
lawsuits and appealed to politicians in attempts to ban it. Campus
Crusade for Christ leader Bill Bright offered $10 million to buy the

Previously published in *Free Inquiry*, Spring 2003.

movie and burn it. Most theaters in the southern United States, fearing savage reprisals, refused to show the film.

All this tumult provided an epitaph for a brilliant, brooding, funny, sad, profound Greek writer who had died three decades earlier. The movie was drawn from his most controversial novel.

Philosopher-author Nikos Kazantzakis was a literary giant who left an indelible mark on the modern world. Born in Crete in 1885 (some references say 1883), he attended a Catholic school then studied law in Athens, later philosophy in Paris under Henri Bergson, the eventual Nobel laureate who focused on the "vital force" of the human spirit.

Fascinated by spiritual questions, Kazantzakis published his first book and play in 1906 while still a student. During ensuing years, he traveled through Europe and Asia, writing dramas, epic verse, and travel books.

In 1917, he and a foreman operated a lignite mine on a Greek island—an experience he later fictionalized in his most renowned novel, *Zorba the Greek*.

In 1919, Kazantzakis was appointed welfare minister of Greece. By the time he resigned in 1927, he had fed and rescued 150,000 Greek residents trapped by a civil war in the Caucasus.

Sympathetic to Marxism, he was a war correspondent during the Spanish Civil War in the 1930s and eventually was awarded the Lenin Peace Prize—but trips to the Soviet Union disillusioned him, and he never joined the Communist Party.

Before World War II, he lived on the Greek island of Aegina. After the war, he married late in life, became a Greek government minister again, then worked for UNESCO. Finally, he and his wife settled at Antibes, France.

Kazantzakis didn't begin writing novels until midlife, but they brought his greatest fame and impact. His *Zorba the Greek* portrayed a bookish young intellectual operating a lignite mine on a Greek island—while learning about life from Zorba, his lusty, crafty, uneducated, smart, exuberant foreman. Zorba danced wildly, laughed at social and religious lunacy, and personified Bergson's "vital force."

Like most agnostic philosophers, Zorba and his young employer tried in vain to discern a meaning in life. The unlettered workman begged his educated companion for answers—then scorned his scholarly learning when he could provide none:

> Zorba looked at the sky with open mouth in a sort of ecstasy, as though he were seeing it for the first time. . . .
>
> "Can you tell me, boss," he said, and his voice sounded deep and earnest in the warm night, "what all these things mean? Who made them all? And why? And, above all"—here Zorba's voice trembled with anger and fear—"why do people die?"
>
> "I don't know, Zorba," I replied, ashamed, as if I had been asked the simplest thing, the most essential thing, and was unable to explain it.
>
> "You don't know!" said Zorba in round-eyed astonishment, just like his expression the night I had confessed that I could not dance. . . . "Well, all those damned books you read—what good are they? Why do you read them? If they don't tell you that, what do they tell you?"
>
> "They tell me about the perplexity of mankind, who can give no answer to the question you've just put to me, Zorba."[1]

Burly Zorba and his egghead "boss" observed absurd religious superstitions of the villagers surrounding them. They laughed at the pretense of priests and the gullibility of believers. Zorba scoffed: "God makes them deaf or blind, and they say: 'God be praised.'"[2]

"But we have no God to nourish us, Zorba," the employer observed.[3]

And Zorba commented:

> "Would God bother to sit over the earthworms and keep count of everything they do? And get angry and storm and fret himself silly because one went astray with the female earthworm next door or swallowed a mouthful of meat on Good Friday? Bah! Get away with you, all you soup-swilling priests! Bah!"[4]

Yet they returned, again and again, to the enigma that haunted them.

> "When a man dies, can he come to life again?" he asked abruptly.
>
> "I don't think so, Zorba."
>
> "Neither do I. . . ."[5]

Zorba urged his employer to pursue a buxom village widow who exuded sensuality. "If you're looking for any other paradise than that, my poor fellow, there is none! Don't listen to what the priests tell you, there's no other!"[6]

Zorba shrewdly perceived that his intellectual friend had little interest in succeeding as a lignite miner—that his real dream was to create a retreat for thinkers and scholars. When their mine failed, and they finally parted, the owner reassured him:

> "Don't fret, Zorba, we shall meet again, and, who knows, man's strength is tremendous! One day we'll put our great plan into effect: we'll build a monastery of our own, without a god, without a devil, but with free men; and you shall be the gatekeeper, Zorba. . . ."[7]

Zorba the Greek was published in 1946, gaining great popularity, and became a successful movie two decades later with Anthony Quinn as the cunning hero. Neither the novel nor the film caused noticeable controversy.

But a later novel, *The Last Temptation of Christ*, printed in 1955, was a bombshell. Multitudes of Christians were outraged by its portrayal of Jesus as uncertain and self-doubting, distracted by his yearning for Mary Magdalene. The Vatican banned the book, and the Greek Orthodox Church excommunicated Kazantzakis, a nominal member. Movie producers avoided the novel—until 1988, when it finally was directed by Catholic-born Martin Scorsese, who cast no Jews in the film to avert bigoted hostility. Even with that precaution, it nonetheless provoked rage.

Kazantzakis received the International Peace Award in Vienna in 1956. He was nominated repeatedly for the Nobel Prize for Literature, and in 1957 he lost by a single vote to Albert Camus. Later that year, he died of leukemia in Germany.

Albert Schweitzer wrote: "Since I was a young boy, no author has made such a deep impression on me as Nikos Kazantzakis. His work has depth and durable value because he has experienced much and in the human community he has suffered and yielded much."[8]

Of dramas Kazantzakis wrote in France, a critic said: "At the center of these plays stands the same figure, a solitary anti-hero, understanding (as the rest of the world does not) that the struggle at the heart of the play's action justifies itself but is inevitably fruitless."[9]

Unable to find ultimate meaning in life, the narrator of *Zorba* contents himself with small treasures: "How simple and frugal a thing is happiness: a glass of wine, a roast chestnut, a wretched little brazier, the sound of the sea."[10]

Kazantzakis saw the perplexity of mankind, who can give no answer to the final riddle.

NOTES

1. Nikos Kazantzakis, *Zorba the Greek* (New York: Simon & Schuster, 1952), p. 269.

2. Ibid., p. 62.

3. Ibid, p. 184.

4. Ibid., p. 234.

5. Ibid., p. 106.

6. Ibid., p. 101.

7. Ibid., p. 298.

8. Albert Schweitzer, quoted in *Twentieth Century Authors, First Supplement* (New York: H. W. Wilson, 1955), p. 515.

9. Christopher Robinson, in *Reader's Encyclopedia of Eastern European Literature* (New York: HarperCollins, 1993), p. 183.

10. Kazantzakis, *Zorba the Greek*, p. 80.

12

ASHCROFT AND
"THE UNKNOWN TONGUE"

N ews reporters are reluctant to inquire about a public figure's religion. They assume that each person's faith is a deeply private matter. Therefore, nobody asked former Missouri Senator John Ashcroft—George W. Bush's choice for US attorney general—about "speaking in tongues."

Hundreds of reports were written about Ashcroft's apparent racism and his extreme-right political beliefs, but the national media were silent on his Pentecostalism.

However, if it's appropriate to print every tiny detail of President Bill Clinton's sex life, I think Americans also are entitled to know that their attorney general practiced a controversial form of worship.

Talking in tongues, or glossolalia, is the heart of the Pentecostal movement, a large phenomenon. Its US adherents outnumber Presbyterians, Episcopalians, Jews, and several other groups. The *Encyclopedia Britannica* estimates its ranks as high as twelve million. It

---

Previously published in the *Charleston Gazette*, January 13, 2001.

involves chiefly the least-educated believers, including those some-times scornfully dubbed "holy rollers."

When I was an Appalachian newspaper religion reporter in the 1950s and '60s, I witnessed "the tongues" hundreds of times, especially at serpent-handling and faith-healing sessions. Here's how it happens.

During an emotional prayer session, a worshiper stands and "testifies," often with arms waving or animated dancing. Suddenly, a torrent of incoherent syllables bursts from the believer's throat—"shend-a-la-goosh-a-ma," or the like. It's usually accompanied by spastic jerking. It's electrifying and often causes others around the room to jerk and spout, contagiously.

I'm sure the worshipers don't do it deliberately. I think they're in a hypnotic state, with little control over the outpouring. They say it's the Holy Ghost speaking through them. The preacher at such a service usually says the congregants are speaking Russian or Chinese of some other "unknown tongue."

(I once read that Asia's "whirling dervishes" make similar "ecstatic utterances" as they dance.)

Christian Pentecostalism is rooted in chapter 2 of the Book of Acts, which says the disciples gathered on the day of Pentecost, when they were engulfed by a "sound from heaven as of a rushing mighty wind" and "there appeared to them cloven tongues like as of fire. . . . And they were all filled with the Holy Ghost, and began to speak with other tongues, as the Spirit gave them utterance."

Glossolalia cropped up among various medieval sects and among America's Shakers in the 1700s. Modern Pentecostalism started in 1900 when a Kansas Bible school teacher urged his stu-dents to fast and pray for the "baptism of the Holy Spirit." Eventu-ally, on New Year's Day 1901, a female student began spouting the sounds, and the phenomenon spread rapidly.

Sometimes it's called the "charismatic" movement. (Charisma is the ability to produce an emotional response in others.) Pente-costalism also stresses divine healing and other supernatural fea-tures, but glossolalia is the key factor.

Over the years, some standard church congregations have encountered "tongues" trouble. A few members, or even the pastor, acquire glossolalia, and other members are repelled. It has caused church splits.

For a while in the 1960s, the custom crept into a few Episcopal churches, and rebel Bishop James Pike of California denounced it. He said it was akin to mental illness. (I covered a national assembly of Episcopal bishops at Oglebay Park in Wheeling, West Virginia, in 1966 as the bishops were preparing to try Pike on heresy charges.)

The Assemblies of God became Pentecostalism's largest branch. The church's Web site claims 2.5 million US members and 29 million others around the world. Senator Ashcroft's father was a major leader of the denomination, and the son followed as its best-known lay member. He has confirmed that he received the "baptism of the Holy Spirit" but declines to say more.

Several national reports have said that Ashcroft's far-right political views arose from his religious faith. Now you know what that faith entails.

13

FEW UNDERSTAND RELIGIOUS FREEDOM

Freedom of religion means the government can't tell you what to believe, which deities to worship, or whether to worship any at all. Each American is free to make a personal, private decision about this profoundly important topic. Politicians and government agencies mustn't do it for you.

Religious freedom is a core guarantee in America's Bill of Rights, locked into the First Amendment. It was drafted by America's visionary founders—Thomas Jefferson, John Adams, James Madison, George Mason, and others—who were horrified by Europe's bloody record of government-enforced religion.

In his *Notes on the State of Virginia*, Jefferson wrote:

Millions of innocent men, women and children, since the introduction of Christianity, have been burnt, tortured, fined, imprisoned, yet we have not advanced one inch toward uniformity. What

Previously published in the *Charleston Gazette*, June 28, 2002.

has been the effect of coercion? To make one half of the world fools and the other half hypocrites.

Mason, Adams, Madison, Thomas Paine, Benjamin Franklin, and even Ethan Allen wrote similar warnings. The only cure, they said, is separation of church and state. Government mustn't try to dictate religion, and churches mustn't try to use government power to impose their beliefs on others.

However, few Americans understand this crucial component of democracy. Instead, the majority endlessly seeks government imposition of belief through school prayer, posting the Ten Commandments in public buildings, banning evolution from science classes, giving tax money to church schools, erecting religious monuments in public parks, and the like. It's a struggle that never ends.

Shrewd politicians see that America is more religious than other democracies—thus they know they can win elections by posing as pious. Proclaiming faith wins votes. Doing the opposite could bring swift defeat.

That's why Congress adopted "In God We Trust" as the US motto in 1956 (after decreeing it for gold and silver coins in 1908 and putting it on paper money in 1955). That's why Congress amended the Pledge of Allegiance in 1954 to declare that America is one nation "under God."

After a federal court ruled that the latter violates the separation of church and state, politicians trumpeted outrage. West Virginia Senator Robert C. Byrd, a Democrat, called the judge who wrote the ruling an "atheist lawyer." Former Senate Majority Leader Tom Daschle, a Democrat from South Dakota, said the court decision was "just nuts." Senator Joseph Lieberman of Connecticut (who is so pious that he won't drive a car on the Sabbath), called it a "senseless, ridiculous decision." Former Attorney General John Ashcroft vowed to fight the court ruling.

Overwhelmingly, members of Congress vowed to alter the Bill of Rights to let the government endorse religion. If they ever put such a constitutional amendment on the national ballot, there's no doubt that Americans would pass it in a landslide.

Personally, I hope such spasms of political piety never succeed in damaging the landmark principle of the founding fathers. That principle already is compromised by other holy political proclamations. Actually, "under God" and "In God We Trust" are mostly lip service. Legendary Justice William Brennan wrote that they are mere "ceremonial deism" and "have lost through rote repetition any significant religious content."

I'm always leery of politicians who broadcast their religion. The more they have to hide, I figure, the louder they pray.

After President Bill Clinton was caught in the Monica mess, he paraded to church each Sunday with a Bible tucked conspicuously under his arm.

While President George W. Bush was taking vast sums from the Enron crooks, he proclaimed "Jesus Day" as governor of Texas and never missed a chance to display sanctimony.

Corrupt politicos in my state of West Virginia were mainstays at prayer breakfasts. In 1988, the top three supplicants at the state's annual legislative prayer breakfast were Governor Arch Moore, Senate President Dan Tonkovich, and visiting Georgia congressman Patrick Swindall. Within a couple of years, all three were in federal prisons.

I don't want pious politicians tampering with America's precious religious freedom.

14

CLASH OF CIVILIZATIONS

Pesident George W. Bush says the war on terror and his Iraq invasion aren't a conflict with Islam. He may be sincere—yet there's another way to view the crisis, based on the long sweep of history.

In one sense, at least partly, the twenty-first-century struggle can be seen as continuing a fourteen-hundred-year "clash of civilizations" between the Muslim East and the Judeo-Christian West—a recurring bloodbath that has killed vast millions. Consider this record.

After Islam began in the early 600s, it unified Arabian tribes into a mighty conquering force. They battled eastward into India and westward across North Africa, spreading the faith as they went, crushing Christian communities. Leaping the Mediterranean, Muslims swept through Spain and fought their way into France, before being halted in a historic battle at Tours in 732. Muslims conquered Sicily and Crete in the 820s.

Previously published in the *Charleston Gazette*, February 12, 2003, and syndicated nationally.

In 1095, Pope Urban II launched a famous Christian counterattack: the First Crusade. "God wills it!" became the war cry as European armies and throngs cut a gory path eastward, finally capturing Jerusalem—only to lose it later. Popes loosed a Second Crusade, and a Third, and Fourth, and so on. Crusading consumed Europe for five centuries, but Muslims always regained the seized territory.

What might be termed the Final Crusade was launched in 1571 by Pope Pius V, who sent a Christian naval armada to destroy a Muslim fleet off Lepanto, Greece. Among the Western wounded was Miguel de Cervantes, later to write *Don Quixote*. (Pius also killed Waldensian Christians in Calabria, Huguenot Christians in France, and heretic Christians through the Inquisition—then was canonized a saint.)

Around the eastern Mediterranean, Byzantine Christians fought off endless Muslim invasions—slowly losing ground. By the 1300s, Muslim Turks were marching northward through the Balkans, defeating Orthodox Serbs in 1389 at Kosovo. In 1452, they conquered Constantinople. In 1683, they besieged Vienna a second time but were driven back with terrible losses.

That was the high mark of Islamic conquest. After a thousand years of advance, humiliating retreat set in. The Renaissance and the Industrial Revolution sent Christendom soaring to spectacular wealth and power—while Muslim countries weakened and declined.

Clashes continued. Conflict between Orthodox Russia and Muslim Turkey over Christian holy places caused the Crimean War in the mid-1800s. Christian Armenians mutinied against Muslim Turkey for generations and finally waged an armed rebellion during World War I—causing a historic slaughter of Armenians. After Armenia became part of the Soviet Union, it plunged into hostility with Muslim Azerbaijan.

Muslim humiliation grew as European colonial forces dominated Islamic lands. In the mid-1800s, France grabbed Algeria and later Tunisia. In the late 1800s, Egypt begged for help in suppressing a Muslim holy war in the upper Nile Valley, and Britain sent battalions with Maxim guns—then later made Egypt a "protectorate," along with Sudan. Early in the 1900s, Iran temporarily came under British and Russian sway. Italy took Libya. Almost every European country seized parts of Morocco. After World War I, Lebanon and

Syria became French colonies, and Britain took control of Iraq, Jordan, and Palestine.

Many scholars have observed that millions of Muslims are resentful because their once-glorious culture stagnated and is brushed off as third-rate by Westerners.

Perhaps the worst affront to the Islamic world occurred after World War II, when Western powers gave Jews a homeland in part of Muslim Palestine. Hate and killing over Israel have ensued ever since. And there's other strife.

Recurring Muslim-Christian warfare in Sudan since the 1950s has killed about two million. In the 1970s, the revolt of Muslim tribes against Russian dominance in Afghanistan might be construed as part of the "clash of civilizations." In the 1980s, Lebanon was shattered by a civil war between militias of Christian and Muslim ethnic groups. In the 1990s, the rupture of former Yugoslavia pitted Muslim and Christian populations against each other. Today, other Christian-Muslim conflicts are raging in Indonesia, Nigeria, the Philippines, and elsewhere.

How much of this ferment derives from the historic fault line between the two cultures—and how much is spawned merely by local hate and regional political disputes? Frankly, I doubt if the world's best scholars could say with certainty. (Plenty of other wars have been fought for entirely different reasons.)

It's oversimplistic to apply bumper-sticker labels to complex international problems. Nonetheless, the great divide between the Judeo-Christian world and the Islamic realm always hovers in the background, affecting opponents.

Some militant mullahs base their entire careers on denouncing "enemies of God," meaning Westerners. And everyone knows that wealthy Osama bin Laden financed an international terror network to utilize this hate. Repeatedly, he has proclaimed that his jihad (holy war) is against "Jews and Crusaders." In his mind, at least, the East-West battlefront is quite clear.

World events can be seen from many perspectives, each correct in its own way. Is President Bush accurate in saying his blitz has nothing to do with Islam? Looking at the fourteen centuries of mayhem, I'm not so sure.

15

THE GREAT
WEST VIRGINIA HOLY WAR

Millionaire evangelists such as Pat Robertson and Jerry Fal-well want America's fifty million fundamentalists to become a mighty political force and reshape society to their liking. Well, the rest of us had better pray that their effort doesn't turn out like a famous West Virginia example: the 1974 Kanawha County war against "godless textbooks." I lived through it—and it was a religious nightmare.

Rock-throwing mobs forced schools to close. Two schools and the board office were bombed. Two people were shot. Coal miners struck to support the religious protest. Ku Klux Klansmen and right-wing kooks flocked to Charleston. A preacher and his followers discussed murdering families who wouldn't join a school boycott. The minister finally went to prison.

During this mess, Charleston acquired a national image somewhat like Dayton, Tennessee, home of the "Scopes monkey trial," the 1925 clash over evolution.

Previously published in the *Charleston Gazette*, October 12, 1993.

Ironically, the whole Kanawha insurrection was pointless because the schoolbooks were just routine texts. Their sins existed only in the fevered imagination of the zealots.

The upheaval was rooted in the period when religious conservatives rebelled against liberal excesses of the 1960s. The first to jump into the limelight was the Rev. Charles Meadows, who went before the state legislature to demand a return of the death penalty. He testified that he would "be glad to pull the switch myself" at executions.

Then he attacked sex education in Kanawha schools. He rented a theater and invited "Bible-believing Christians" to a rally against the "pornography" of sex education. Committees were formed. A movement grew.

Alice Moore, wife of a fundamentalist pastor, became the movement's candidate for the school board. She said sex education was part of a "humanistic, atheistic attack on God." Church groups poured money into her campaign. She won and became the board's ayatollah, supporting Bibles for students and expulsion of pregnant girls.

Moore's moralizing had minor effect until 1974, when new textbooks were up for adoption. She denounced the books as irreligious, and a protest grew. A group of twenty-seven born-again clergymen called the texts "immoral and indecent." (Rascals like me hunted for indecency in the books but found only ordinary school topics.)

On the night of the adoption vote, a thousand protesters surrounded the board office. Despite this menace, members voted 3–2 for the books. Afterward, a group called Christian American Parents picketed stores owned by a board member who voted yes.

When school opened, evangelists urged "true Christians" to keep their children home. Attendance fell 20 percent—more so in the poor eastern end of the county. The Rev. Marvin Horan led a rally of two thousand protesters in a coal-mining hollow. Mobs surrounded schools and blockaded school bus garages. Teachers were threatened. So were families who didn't join the boycott.

About thirty-five hundred coal miners went on strike against the texts and began picketing Charleston industries. Flying rocks, screams, and danger were constant. Frightened people began carrying pistols. Many school buses couldn't run—and then textbook pickets halted city buses, leaving eleven thousand low-income folks without transportation.

Pickets surrounded a truck terminal, and a terminal janitor fired a shot that wounded one. Other pickets beat the janitor savagely. The next day, an armed man panicked when pickets surged toward him. He fired a shot that wounded a bystander. Two book protesters were jailed for smashing windshields.

The school board got a court injunction against disrupters, but it didn't help. Finally the superintendent closed schools, saying the safety of children couldn't be guaranteed. Schools also closed in two adjoining counties.

Network TV crews swarmed to Charleston. A cameraman was trounced by protesters at a rally. The Rev. Ezra Graley led a march on the state capitol and filed a federal suit against the textbooks. Graley and other ministers were jailed for contempt of the court injunction.

Schools reopened. The boycott resumed. The Rev. Charles Quigley prayed for God to kill the board members who endorsed the books. A grade school was hit by a Molotov cocktail. Five shots hit a school bus. A dynamite blast damaged another grade school. A bigger blast damaged the school central office.

Near-riot conditions continued. Robert Dornan of California, a pornography foe who later became a right-wing extremist in Congress, addressed a crowd of three thousand. Protesters started born-again schools. A magistrate led an attempt to make the Bible-believing eastern region a separate county.

Minister Horan and three of his followers were indicted for the bombings. Ku Klux Klan leaders led a Charleston rally to support them. An imperial wizard from Georgia said the Kanawha textbooks contained "the most vulgar, vile, and filthy words in print"— which was odd, since nonfundamentalists couldn't find any obscenities in them.

During the trial in 1975, other followers said Horan had led the dynamite plot, telling them there was "a time to kill." They said the plotters talked of wiring dynamite caps into the gas tanks of cars in which families were driving their children to school during the boycott. This willingness to burn parents and kids to death for religious purposes showed the fundamentalist mind in all its sickness. All four defendants went to federal prison.

Horan's conviction ended the protest. Other leaders lost face. Minister Meadows left his church after admitting involvement with a woman religion teacher. Minister Graley's wife left him, and he sued to recover the luxury car she took. School board member Moore abruptly left the state.

Looking back, it was a season of madness—a frenzy over nothing, like the ferment among believers who thought the moon-and-stars logo on Procter & Gamble soap was a secret sign of Satan. The chaos showed how zealots can turn trivia into tragedy.

16

THE CODE OF THE UNIVERSE

Electrons and quarks, galaxies and black holes, electromagnetic radia-
tion, DNA and cells, gravity, molecular bonds, the speed of light, the
power in the nucleus—these contain a gospel more profound than any
written by humans.

D id you know that Albert Einstein, although Jewish, went
through a brief childhood phase of devout Christianity?
In an autobiographical sketch written at age sixty-seven, he
described his short-lived faith, planted in him by daily indoctrina-
tion at a Catholic school to which his parents had sent him:

> Thus I came—despite the fact that I was the son of entirely irreli-
> gious (Jewish) parents—to a deep religiosity, which, however,
> found an abrupt ending at the age of 12. Through the reading of
> popular scientific books, I soon reached the conviction that much
> in the stories of the Bible could not be true.

Previously published in *The Humanist,* September-October 1988.

The consequence was a positively fanatic freethinking, coupled with the impression that youth is intentionally being deceived by the state through lies. It was a crushing impression.

Suspicion against every kind of authority grew out of this experience, a skeptical attitude toward the convictions which were alive in any specific social environment—an attitude which has never left me, even though later on, because of a better insight into the causal connections, it lost some of its original poignancy.

It is quite clear to me that the religious paradise of youth, which was thus lost, was a first attempt to free myself from the chains of the "merely personal," from an existence which is dominated by wishes, hopes and primitive feelings. Out yonder there was this huge world, which exists independently of us human beings and which stands before us like a great, eternal riddle, at least partially accessible to our inspection and thinking. The contemplation of this world beckoned like a liberation. . . .

The road to this paradise was not as comfortable and alluring as the road to the religious paradise, but it has proved itself as trustworthy, and I have never regretted having chosen it.[1]

Commenting on Einstein's reminiscence, physicist Heinz Pagels wrote:

What this passage reveals is a conversion from personal religion to the "cosmic religion" of science, an experience which changed him for the rest of his life. Einstein saw that the universe is governed by laws that can be known by us but that are independent of our thoughts and feelings. The existence of this cosmic code—the laws of material reality as confirmed by experience—is the bedrock faith that moves the natural scientist. The scientist sees in that code the eternal structure of reality, not as imposed by man or tradition but as written into the very substance of the universe. This recognition of the nature of the universe can come as a profound and moving experience to the young mind.[2]

Looking into the soul of the universe isn't just for world-class physicists. It can happen to anyone who ponders the awesome discoveries of science, from quarks to quasars.

When I was a farm boy in West Virginia, my grandfather taught me the orbits of Earth and the moon, and I thought it was utterly amazing that these colossal balls weighing quintillions of tons were whirling and circling and rolling forever in open space—and that we live on one of them.

When I studied chemistry in high school and learned the combining valences of atoms, I thought it was utterly amazing that this hidden code governs virtually all matter—Earth and the moon, our bodies, trees, water, air. How could atoms lock together into substances because of gaps in their outer layers of electrons—electrons eternally streaking at nearly the speed of light?

Why do the mysterious electrical parts of atoms whirl forever, like the planets and stars?

Why do electrically neutral atoms seize onto each other, just because their outer electrons lack the magic number of eight?

Why do they turn into remarkably different things as they combine? Hydrogen gas and oxygen gas are nothing like water, yet they constitute it. Some carbon atoms lock in tetrahedrons to become diamonds; others lock in layers of six-sided carbon rings to become graphite pencil lead.

Why do atoms link into carbon-based molecules that link into amino acids that link into proteins that link into living cells as complex as whole cities—and why does all this link into a thinking, feeling, loving, fearing, aging, dying human?

How can a combination of amino acids write a symphony or join the Republican Party or commit stock fraud or feel patriotism for a section of Earth likewise composed of molecules?

The old "planetary" model of the atom was envisioned like a solar system—orbits around a nucleus. This raised a far-out theory that our solar system might be an atom in some stupefyingly larger universe, that our atoms might be tiny solar systems with people living on some of the particles. I first encountered this idea in a Captain Marvel comic book.

The great astronomer Harlow Shapley once gave a talk at West Virginia State College. I hung around afterward and asked him, "What's the name of the theory that atoms might be solar systems?" He looked at me and said, "The name of it is damn nonsense." I later learned that it's called the subatomic universe theory—but Shapley's name probably is better.

During this period, when I was muddling over the boggling

impossibilities that science revealed, I started reading books on Einstein and relativity and found that his scientific truth was even more astonishing. What our common sense tells us is real can't be real if space shrinks to nonexistence or time runs slower and stops under some conditions.

I hatched mental experiments that short-circuited my brain. For example, Einstein says the speed of light is the great constant of the universe—nothing can go faster. He also says all speeds are relative between moving objects. Well, if you strike a match, photons of visible light fly out in all directions. If one photon is going west at the speed of light and another is going east at the speed of light, how fast are they separating from each other?

It gets even worse when you read quantum physics. The more I studied, the more I developed an eerie sense that the world we think we inhabit and all existing things are some sort of fiction.

For example, take steel. It can be a hundred-foot bridge girder or it can be the coil of a bass piano string, a long wire spiraled into a hard spring. All the curves of that spring are composed of iron atoms locked rigidly to each other in a strong crystal lattice that is nearly unbreakable.

Yet those atoms are an illusion of emptiness. They are a void of unknowable electrical charges. They are virtually a vacuum. They are as empty as the solar system. If you look at the night sky and see how remote the planets are, that's how remote the parts of an atom are from each other.

If an atom were the size of a fourteen-story building, the nucleus would be a grain of salt in the middle of the seventh floor, too tiny to be seen. Therefore, heavy, rigid steel doesn't exist the way we think it does. It's 99.999999 percent vacuum—as empty as the night sky.

Sometimes I picture atoms as soap bubbles: empty but bumping against each other and sticking together. The buzzing outer electrons are negative, and they repel the negative electron clouds of adjoining atoms. This holds the atoms apart and gives them an illusion of solidity. Yet they are bound to each other by valence bonds and hydrogen bonds and Van der Waals bonds and other electrical links.

Atom emptiness is the key to white dwarfs, pulsars, and black holes.

At the end of their life cycles, stars explode. Then, what's left of them collapses, and gravity pulls the collapsing material into incredible density. If the residue is small, compressed electrons in the seething stellar plasma of crushed atoms push back fiercely and resist further collapse. This produces a white dwarf that is nearly impossible to comprehend. The material of a white dwarf weighs around ten tons per thimbleful. How could something the size of a thimble be so heavy that a hundred strong men couldn't lift it? It might crush a house. A large crane would be required to pick it up.

But that's just the first step in removing the empty space inside atoms. A teenage genius, Subrahmanyan Chandrasekhar, computed that, if a collapsing star has 1.4 times the mass of our sun, its gravity would be too great to be stopped by the resistance of the electrons. He didn't know it, but he was predicting pulsars, or neutron stars, which later were discovered. Their enormous gravity squeezes the electrons into the nucleus of each atom, where they merge with protons to form a solid mass of neutrons. This material weighs about ten million tons per cubic centimeter. A c.c. is the size of a bouillon cube. Can you imagine a bouillon cube weighing more than the Empire State Building? But that's what matter is when the empty space is removed between the nucleus and the electrons of atoms.

If ten million tons of actual substance is the size of a bouillon cube, how much real material is in a 180-pound man or a 120-pound woman? Not as much as a dust speck. Not enough to see with a microscope. Our five-foot or six-foot bodies, like all material things, are an illusion made of vacuum and whirling electrical charges.

It gets worse. Even the packed neutrons in a pulsar are not basic material. They, too, are empty and compressible. If the remains of a collapsing star are 3.2 times as large as our sun, the gravity is too strong to be checked at the pulsar level. The collapse continues until it passes the point of no return—the Schwarzchild radius—and becomes a black hole, the ultimate pit of gravity, where everything is compressed to nothing.

If planet Earth were squeezed to its Schwarzchild radius, it would be the size of a pearl. Can anyone imagine the matter of the entire Earth being reduced to fingernail size—but retaining all its weight—and continuing to shrink beyond that point?

This isn't Captain Marvel comics. Pulsars are real. So are black holes, the astrophysicists say. If they are actuality, then what is our everyday world?

The nonreality of matter is just one of many enigmas that science reveals. Consider these:

- As we lie "still" in bed, we are flying sixty-seven thousand miles an hour around the sun and six hundred thousand miles an hour around the Milky Way galaxy.

- When we see the North Star, we are looking back in time to the medieval era because the light we see began traveling 680 years ago.

- Every second, the visible universe expands by a volume as large as the Milky Way.

- Peaceful atoms of rock, lying still for centuries, have a power in their nuclei that is beyond comprehension: Only as much matter as a dime was transformed into the energy that destroyed Hiroshima and killed 140,000 people.

- The smallness of atoms likewise is beyond grasping: A cubic inch of air contains three hundred billion billion molecules, all moving at a thousand miles an hour and hitting each other five billion times a second.

- Although atoms are generally indestructible, their electrons keep coming loose to produce lightning and the other electricity of the world.

- The light we see, the sun warmth we feel, the radio and television signals we receive, the x-rays we use—all of these come from electrons. Photons of electromagnetic radiation are emitted by excited electrons oscillating or dropping to lower layers in atoms.

- Most life on Earth comes from a tiny electric current: When sunlight hits chlorophyll molecules, excited outer electrons jump through a mosaic of molecules, and this energy drives plant processes.

- As for the DNA that conveys our genetic code, there is six feet of it inside each cell of our bodies. The body has more than ten trillion cells, so every person contains several billion miles of DNA.

- The "spin" of electrons is so powerful it can suspend railway locomotives in the air (in "maglev," or magnetic levitation, trains). Electrons of most atoms are in balanced pairs with opposite spin, so the atoms have no magnetism. But ferrous atoms have a few electrons that aren't balanced, giving each atom a magnetic field. When an electrical current induces all the atoms in a piece of iron to align their polarity in unison, a strong electromagnet is created.

These amazing realities are profoundly important, yet, when I try to discuss science with my chums in the news business or music circles or political groups, they look at me as if I'm babbling in the Unknown Tongue. They are highly educated people who know multitudes of facts, but they shrug at what I think are the most crucial facts of all.

If philosophy is an attempt to comprehend the universe and the meaning of life, then science is the best portal. Every time I learn another rule of subatomic forces or cell behavior or galactic motion, I get an eerie sense of glimpsing the mysterious code underlying our existence. Physicists often apply the word God to this order, but they don't mean God in the church sense.

In a world of supernatural religions, mystical religions, guilt-based religions, violent religions, money-collecting religions, social club religions, and cult religions, grasping the code of the universe is the most religious experience I know.

NOTES

1. Albert Einstein, from "Autobiographical Notes," in *Albert Einstein Philosopher-Scientist* (1946), quoted in Heinz R. Pagels, *The Cosmic Code: Quantum Physics as the Language of Nature* (New York: Simon & Schuster, 1982; New York: Bantam, 1983), p. 7.

2. Pagels, *The Cosmic Code*, p. 8.

17

THE BEAST IN THE
SHADOWS BEHIND RELIGION

I n the newspaper business, we deal in reality every day. Here's a reality of religion, as it comes across the news wires:

2,000 DIE IN RIOTS AFTER HINDUS SMASH MUSLIM MOSQUE
ULSTER CATHOLIC, PROTESTANT SQUADS TRADE MURDERS
OHIO CULT LEADER 'SACRIFICES' FAMILY OF FIVE
ORTHODOX CHRISTIAN SERBS RAPE MUSLIM WOMEN
SHIITES IN IRAN HANG BAHAIS WHO WON'T CONVERT
CHRISTIAN ARMENIANS, MUSLIM AZERBAIJANIS RESUME WAR
FUNDAMENTALIST PICKET KILLS CLINIC DOCTOR
BUDDHISTS AND HINDU TAMILS BATTLE IN SRI LANKA
EGYPTIAN FUNDAMENTALISTS KILL PRESIDENT SADAT
SIKH MILITANTS ASSASSINATE INDIRA GANDHI
JEWISH FUNDAMENTALIST KILLS PRIME MINISTER RABIN
900 TAKE CYANIDE AT JONESTOWN
CHRISTIAN-MUSLIM WAR IN SUDAN CAUSES FAMINE

Previously published in the *Charleston Gazette*, April 21, 1993, and syndicated nationally; and in *Free Inquiry*, Summer 1993, and *Freethought Today*, June-July 1993.

WACO CULTISTS DIE IN SUICIDE PYRE
'MARTYRS' CRASH PLANES INTO WORLD TRADE CENTER

And so forth.

At an editors' conference in Baltimore, actress Shirley MacLaine lamented:

> In the name of God, a 'fatwa' against Salman Rushdie. In the name of God, murder in the Balkans. In the name of God, the bombing of the World Trade Center. In the name of God, the siege at Waco, Texas. . . . In the name of God, Shiites and Sunnis are at each other's throats in Iraq and Iran, as are Arabs and Jews in the Middle East. . . . In the name of God, what is going on?

What's going on is an aspect of religion the world avoids discussing—the Mr. Hyde lurking behind Dr. Jekyll.

Everyone knows the good face of faith. In my city, for instance, an Episcopal church serves "manna meals" to the down-and-out, the Samaritan Inn provides shelter for the homeless, the Salvation Army cares for winos, the Mountain Mission gives furniture and clothes to the needy, the Covenant House works daily with street people, Catholic volunteers repair poor people's homes in rural hollows, churches run many food-banks for the jobless.

All these things reinforce the universal belief that religion makes believers kind and caring. But what can explain the opposite result?

As for the holy wars between ethnic groups, scholars and historians say the hatred isn't religious, it's cultural and political and economic. They're right—but they're wrong. It's true that many factors mingle in any human conflict, yet the chief dividing element in some horrors is faith.

In Northern Ireland, how would two residents of Belfast know they're enemies if they didn't go to different churches? They look, speak, and dress alike. They live in similar houses. Why don't their families intermarry, work together, socialize together, and forget ancient grudges? Because religion keeps them alienated in hostile camps. "Religious tribalism" is a name applied to it.

In Bosnia, next-door neighbors equally alike suddenly began killing each other. Why? Because they pray to different gods. Otherwise, there would be no way to distinguish between the neighbors.

Religion-based gore has been recurring for at least nine centuries. When Europe's Crusaders marched off to rid the Holy Land of infidels, they first paused to slaughter "the infidel among us," Jews living in Germany. The Holy Inquisition burned at least two hundred thousand women in the historic witch hunts. The Reformation triggered scores of Catholic-Protestant wars, including the Thirty Years' War, which killed half the population of Germany. England's Puritans and Anglicans waged ferocious combat. Anabaptists were executed by both Protestants and Catholics for the crime of double baptism.

A few years ago, I wrote what evidently was the world's first book on religious atrocities of all types, *Holy Horrors*. Later, people asked why I just chronicled the massacres instead of explaining why they occurred. But who can explain the irrational?

Why do ardent Sikhs gun down Hindu wedding parties to establish "the Land of the Pure"?

Why did medieval inquisitors think two hundred thousand women were copulating with Satan and execute them for it?

Why did the Waco cultists burn their children alive instead of walking out the door?

God only knows. All that can be said with certainty is that there's a beast in the shadows behind religion, and it lunges out periodically, trampling religion's message of compassion.

18

CROOKS, QUACKS, KOOKS, CREEPS, AND CRUDS IN THE CLERGY

Give me that old-time religion . . ."

Pentecostal evangelist Mario Leyva of Columbus, Georgia, sodomized more than a hundred church boys. He was sentenced to twenty years in federal prison. Two assistant pastors got fifteen and twelve years for transporting the boys state-to-state for orgies.

"Give me that old-time religion . . ."

The Rev. Roy Yanke of Beverly Hills, Michigan, pleaded guilty to robbing fourteen banks of $47,000 to pay for his daily use of prostitutes. He got seven years in prison.

"Give me that old-time religion . . ."

Some four hundred US Catholic priests have been charged with child molesting, and the church has paid an estimated $400 million in damages and costs. One priest, James Porter, abused perhaps one hundred victims in three states—including a boy in a full-body cast who couldn't move to resist.

Previously published in *The Humanist*, July-August 1993.

"It's good enough for me . . ."

Born-again con-artist Michael Douglas of Antioch, Illinois, who specialized in investments for wealthy fundamentalists, got a twelve-year sentence for swindling 131 people out of $31 million.

"It was good for Paul and Silas . . ."

Army chaplain aide Steven Ritchie of Fort Lewis, Washington, was sentenced to twenty-six years in prison for raping a six-week-old baby girl.

"It was good for Paul and Silas . . ."

Radio evangelist Willie Winters of Kalamazoo, Michigan, already serving two life terms for a shooting spree, was indicted again on charges of killing his brother-in-law for $22,000 in insurance money.

"It was good for Paul and Silas . . ."

The Rev. Jerry Wilson of Monticello, Indiana, who said his preaching came "from God Himself," had a sexual affair with his secretary at the Bible Tabernacle Church and planted a bomb to kill her husband. Wilson was sentenced to 108 years in prison.

"And it's good enough for me."

*   *   *

I'm a newspaper editor. Day after day I watch the carnival of life via the news wires. To me, the most fascinating oddities in the show are those self-righteous men who say God called them to cleanse impurities from others.

I'm leery of people who talk to invisible beings—but at least some in the praying set are kind and tolerant. The unkind ones demand laws to use the police power of the state to make everyone obey their taboos. They hate sex, and they're relentless in demanding censorship of movies and magazines, condemning unwed mothers and homosexuals, denouncing sex education and birth-control programs.

They attained a pinnacle at the 1992 Republican convention when millionaire evangelists Pat Robertson and Jerry Falwell hailed the GOP's endorsement of their agenda. Right-winger Patrick Buchanan was correct when he told the Republican delegates: "There is a religious war going on in this country for the soul of

America." The war waxes and wanes but never ceases. Endlessly, the issue is whether all Americans will be forced to live by the strictures of those who think they are morally superior.

*   *   *

"It was good for the Hebrew children . . ."

Evangelist Don McCary of Chattanooga, Tennessee, drew a seventy-two-year prison sentence for sodomizing four boys. His twin brother, Christian comedian Ron McCary, is in prison for raping a six-year-old boy. Their older brother, the Rev. Richard McCary, previously was imprisoned for child molesting.

"It was good for the Hebrew children . . ."

The Rev. Richard Snipstead of Minnesota, president of a fundamentalist Lutheran group that denounces homosexuals, confessed that he'd had twenty years of gay relationships, that he carried the AIDS virus, and that he gave the disease to his wife.

"It's that old-time religion . . ."

Catholic priest William Joffe of Milwaukee was jailed for embezzling $264,000 from his parish.

"And it's good enough for me."

Fountain of Life evangelist Jim Whittington of Greenville, North Carolina, was indicted on charges of swindling a paraplegic woman out of $900,000. He called the federal charge an attack "on the gospel of the Lord Jesus Christ."

"It makes you love everybody . . ."

The Rev. Duane Smith, who operated a born-again Christian school in LaPorte, Indiana, got a twelve-year prison term for molesting pupils.

"It makes you love everybody . . ."

The Rev. James Weller of Redwood, California, was convicted of twenty-seven forcible sex crimes against children, some only ten years old. He drew forty-six years in prison.

"It's that old-time religion . . ."

Church deacon Henry Meinholtz, fifty-three, of Kingston, Massachusetts, was convicted of raping and suffocating a thirteen-year-old girl.

"And it's good enough for me."

*   *   *

Many years ago, when I was a young thinker and knew everything, it seemed clear to me that magical, moralistic religion soon would disappear because people were becoming too educated for such superstition.

So much for young thinkers. The opposite occurred. Puritanical fundamentalism not only survived, it rose to dominance in America. Mainline Protestant churches with university-educated clergy are dying, losing members by millions. But the born-again realm is booming.

(Think of the farce at the GOP convention: The president and the ruling party respectfully listened to evangelist Robertson, who claims that his prayers can deflect hurricanes—who wrote in a book that the Gulf War was part of a satanic plot to establish "the New World Order of the Antichrist"—and who wrote that the equal rights movement "encourages women to leave their husbands, kill their children, practice witchcraft, destroy capitalism and become lesbians." Loonies like this aren't taken seriously in other modern nations.)

America has an unwritten rule that all religion must be "respected"—never subjected to public scoffing. But an ugly tide of sex offenses and other crimes by ministers is eroding this code of silence.

Los Angeles Times religion columnist Russell Chandler did research in 1990 and found two thousand cases of sex molestation by clergy pending in the courts. John Cleary, general counsel of Church Mutual Insurance Co., which covers ministers, said: "Today, the number of credible sexual abuse and misconduct cases is astounding."

Some of these men are among the moralizers seeking to jail sellers of sexy videos and books, halt Medicaid abortions for poor girls, and impose state-mandated prayer upon schoolchildren. The hypocrisy is galling.

Old-time religion is having a heyday in America. Its champions seek to dictate behavior rules for all of us—to take away our freedom to make choices for ourselves. We must fight back. We should look at the bizarre array of pontificators and say the obvious:

These preachers are not morally superior to us. In fact, they are inferior, and it is insulting for them to tell us how to live.

19

MY NAME IS JEAN-PAUL SARTRE

Good evening. My name is Jean-Paul Sartre. Students in tonight's audience may be too young to remember me, but you of middle years will recall that I caused great controversy in the era after World War II and was the target of many denunciations.

I want to assure you that, regardless of what you've heard, my life had a beneficial goal: I sought to help people understand the reality of their individual lives amid the world's chaos and madness, and to impress upon them the importance of struggling to improve the human condition.

My message was simple: We are born into an unfathomable existence that has no discernible cosmic or divine purpose—a life often absurd or horrible—and the only valid values are the ones we create for ourselves.

Existence—the reality that engulfs us—is the heart of my philos-

---

Delivered as a lecture at the University of Charleston on November 20, 1991, in a series of speakers impersonating their favorite philosophers.

ophy of existentialism. Existence is all there is, and we must look at it with the clinical eye of the scientist.

Human behavior is a bizarre jumble of affection and hostility, greed and generosity, violence and gentleness. The Chinese concept of the yin and yang—good and evil mixed in each personality—correctly describes the human psyche. The world abounds with love and with horror. People are capable of terrible cruelties to each other. Your modern America has twenty-three thousand murders a year, and a hundred thousand rapes—mostly for no logical reason. "Hell is other people" is a key line in one of my plays.

Meanwhile, random luck governs much of life. Chance gives some people wealth, or intellect, or health—while others are born to misery and early death. By sheer happenstance, some are privileged Americans and some are starving Ethiopians. In the third world, forty thousand children die of malnourishment every day, and the prosperous northern world doesn't even notice.

There is no Grand Order of life. There is no God putting people on Earth as a testing place, consigning the wicked to hell and the righteous to heaven. Such supernatural beliefs are infantile—and the fact that billions of people hold them and worldwide churches promulgate them, merely shows the superstition of the species. (Over the centuries, millions of people have killed each other for their religious beliefs and performed human sacrifices to nonexistent gods. What further proof is needed of the insanity lurking like a monster within our kind?)

On a more logical plane, many people believe there is a "human nature," a universal essence that makes us crave kindness and renounce cruelty. But we existentialists disagree. We think people simply are born as biological creatures, and subsequent conditioning by family and culture shapes each person's nature. "Existence precedes essence" is a fundamental principle of our philosophy.

The universe is indifferent to you and me. There is no "right and wrong" apart from human needs. If a thug rapes and kills a woman on a riverbank, the stream doesn't care. If a child dies of diphtheria, it is of no concern to the diphtheria microbes. If ten thousand Macedonians in full battle array massacre occupants of a Greek city—or if America's "smart" bombs kill two hundred thousand Iraqis—the sun continues to shine on both the killers and the killed.

Yet "right and wrong" are crucial human contrivances—agreed-upon rules to prevent pain and enhance life. What we do may not matter to the universe, but it matters to our fellows.

Since we are born into a world that has no God dictating the rules, or even a biological essence governing behavior, every thinking person is utterly alone in choosing how to live. "Man is condemned to be free" is my phrase for this situation. Despite all the conditioning influences that shape us, it finally is up to each individual, alone, to decide his or her actions. Even when we ask others to guide us, we are making a personal choice. To ask a priest for advice is to choose religion; to ask an agnostic professor is to choose humanism. We cannot avoid choosing a course—even to do nothing is a choice. "Radical freedom" is a label applied to this condition. "There is no reality except in action," I often contended. And we cannot escape the consequences of our actions.

"Abandonment," "anguish," and "despair" are words central to atheistic existentialism—but they are not as morbid as you may think. Abandonment simply means there is no God, thus we are left alone to seek a path. Anguish is the anxiety we feel when we realize that we bear sole responsibility for our actions, and we cannot avoid acting. Despair is the realization that we can rely only upon ourselves—that others who share our beliefs may turn in directions that leave us.

Despite all the uncertainty and futility of life, every person must develop individual integrity and strive to improve the lot of humanity. There are no divine or universal laws—yet we must adopt private values and pursue them. This is the only "authentic" life. It can be expressed this way:

- Never stop advocating reason—even though nine hundred residents of Jonestown swallow cyanide and give it to their children.

- Never stop seeking fairness and decency—even though right-wing death squads rape and decapitate women in El Salvador. (The name of the country, "The Savior," illustrates the irrationality of life.)

- Never stop trying to resolve differences between peoples through logical negotiation—even though more than a hundred local wars have been fought since World War II, with terrible suffering.

- Never stop believing that men and women need each other and that children need parents—even though half of marriages splinter in bitterness, and two thousand American men beat their women to death annually.

- Never stop supporting the freedom of people to follow whatever religion they prefer, or none—even though Shi'ite Muslims in Iran hang Baha'i teenagers who won't convert, or Catholic terrorists machine-gun Protestants in church in Ireland, or Sikhs assassinate Hindus to establish "the Land of the Pure."

- Never stop seeking social justice—even though Texas policemen drown Mexicans in canals, or Los Angeles officers club black speeders.

Although we see madness and cruelty in the fabric of human living, thinking people have a duty to work incessantly to counteract them. If we fail to do so, we allow evil to prevail. Even though we know that death lies ahead for us, and we realize that all our best efforts may come to nothing, we must try. This is "engagement."

One of your modern movies, *Oh God*, bore an agnostic, humanist message: The fictional creator said, "You have everything here on Earth that you need to make life good. Now it is up to you to make it work." This is the obligation of an existentialist—or any person who cares about humanity.

The foregoing summarizes the beliefs I preached in those heady postwar years. Now a word about myself and how I came to my role.

I was born in Paris in 1905, an only child. My father, a naval officer, died when I was a baby. My mother—part of a scholarly family and a niece of the great doctor/humanitarian/musician Albert Schweitzer—brought me to live in the home of her father, a professor at the Sorbonne.

I was small and homely, with eyes that could not focus. I had no playmates. My mother took me to parks, and we roamed from group to group, but none accepted me. Finally, I retreated to our sixth-floor apartment, "on the height where dreams dwell," and sank into the magical world of books and ideas.

I did well in school and was chosen for the prestigious Superior Normal College in the 1920s. There, I became leader of a circle of intense students who met in my room. And it was there that I met Simone de Beauvoir, a brilliant student who had no chance to marry in bourgeois French society because her family was too poor for a dowry. She and I became lovers and settled into a partnership that lasted throughout our lives (although I occasionally exercised an option to have "contingent loves").

I was deeply influenced by two German philosophers: Edmund Husserl, who said it is futile for philosophers to debate abstract principles, and Martin Heidegger, who saw that humans occupy an incomprehensible world, doomed to die without ever knowing why we are here.

After graduation in 1929, I taught in schools of Le Havre, Laon, and finally Paris. In 1938, I published my first novel, *Nausea*, the diary of a tormented man alienated from the physical world, even from his body. In 1939, I was drafted for the new war with Germany and spent a year in a German prison camp. Upon being freed in 1941, I resumed teaching and writing. In 1943, I published *Being and Nothingness*, asserting that the mind, consisting of nothing physical, escapes the deterministic rules that apply to matter.

After the war, my teachings about the senselessness of life became an international sensation. The horrors of the war—and the systematic extermination of six million Jews for the "crime" of deriving from a different religious culture—were powerful proof of my message.

"When it comes to the absurdity of existence," a popular journal said, "war is a great convincer." (Yet proof had been abundant before World War II. Millions of preceding Jews had been killed by Europe's Christians—when they weren't busy killing Muslims in the Crusades, or killing fellow Christians in the Reformation, or torturing heretics in the Inquisition, or burning women in the witch hunts. And there had been wars beyond number. Illogical savagery abounds in history.)

By the 1950s, existentialism was a world craze, changing Western culture. "Theater-of-the-absurd" plays, "antihero" novels, "new wave" movies, and the like contradicted the traditional mythology of noble heroes defeating evil villains. The "new morality" of less-certain values invaded religion. The furor took on dimensions that I scarcely recognized and that I disowned.

I ceased teaching and spent the rest of my life writing. I continued my exhortations for engagement. I advocated a form of Marxism as the best plan for human welfare—yet I refused to join the French Communist Party and was horrified by Soviet cruelties. The world craze faded, and my influence diminished. It resurged briefly in 1964 when I was awarded the Nobel Prize for Literature—but I rejected it, the only person ever to do so, because it represented the bourgeois trappings of success I had long opposed. "A writer must refuse to allow himself to be transformed into an institution," I told the Nobel committee.

In the 1970s, my faulty eyesight failed entirely, my health deteriorated, and I lost the ability to write. "I have lost my reason for being," I told friends. The end came in 1980, at age seventy-four. I hope that I have left behind a basic truth for others to understand. I never preached despair, or felt it, although the vocabulary of existentialism is gloomy. I advocated courageous action seeking to triumph over the abyss. I leave you with a summary thought: "Man can count on no one but himself; he is alone, abandoned on Earth in the midst of his infinite responsibilities, without help, with no other aim than the one he sets for himself, with no other destiny than the one he forges for himself on this Earth."

20

THE EVOLUTION DEBATE IS ABOUT HONESTY

Repeatedly, a visiting "creation scientist" from California challenged me to debate because I support the teaching of evolution. A talk-radio host blistered me on the air because I wouldn't come on his show and quarrel with the creationist professor.

But I felt it would be silly for me to argue about his supernatural beliefs.

After all, I wouldn't debate a Scientologist who asserts that all human souls are "thetans" from another planet. And I wouldn't quarrel with a Unification Church member's claim that Jesus appeared to Master Moon and told him to convert all people as "Moonies." And I wouldn't dispute a Mormon's belief that Jesus visited prehistoric America. And so forth.

Let them all believe whatever they want. It's pointless to go on radio shows and wrangle over mystical claims. However, such claims mustn't be imposed on captive children in government-owned

Previously published in the *Charleston Gazette*, December 21, 1999.

schools. That's prohibited by the separation of church and state, a core principle in the First Amendment in America's Bill of Rights.

America's time-tested freedom of religion means that every group may worship however it wishes in its own private church, but it cannot use the power of government to push its beliefs on others. Therefore, it's always gratifying when school boards rebuff attempts to let creationist teachers denounce evolution in class. Educated families owe thanks to brave board members who withstand pressure from fundamentalists.

To me, the whole issue hinges on honesty. Science, from a Latin word meaning "knowledge," is simply a search for trustworthy facts. It's human intelligence at work. The process is honest because every researcher's claim is challenged by other researchers. They test and retest by many methods until a new idea fails or holds firm. (A researcher who falsifies data is a loathsome criminal in the eyes of fellow scientists.)

While some individual scientists are pig-headed, an entire field cannot be. Science goes where the evidence leads. Science is honest enough to admit mistakes. When new evidence shatters a previous assertion, the old belief is dropped or modified. No such setbacks have hit the theory of evolution.

After 150 years of research, virtually the entire scientific world now agrees that evolution is a fundamental aspect of nature. Complex animals and plants arose from earlier, simpler ones over hundreds of millions of years. The fossil record shows it. Geological strata show it. Radioactive dating shows it. The incredible diversity of species, with variations in different locales, shows it. The uncanny similarity of organs, bones, fluids, and nerves in many animals shows it.

Evolution was proved when skimpy Indian maize was improved into today's nutritious corn. It was proved when drug-resistant bacteria grew from survivors of antibiotic treatment (survival of the fittest). It was proved when England's white moths were gobbled from soot-covered trees by birds, while less visible black variations survived. It was proved by the clear fossil record that today's horse grew from a tiny precursor.

College biology books are filled with many more examples. All this is why evolution should be taught in public school classes along with astronomy, physics, chemistry, and other established sciences. However, a fringe of "creation scientists"—rigid religious zealots—

contend that evolution never happened because it disagrees with their literal reading of the Book of Genesis. These people aren't objective about evidence; they reject anything that supports evolution and exaggerate anything that might concur with the Old Testament.

Ever since the 1925 Scopes Monkey Trial, narrow-thinking American believers have been trying to ban evolution from schools. They think the universe was created in six actual days, as scripture says, with planet Earth and its vegetation formed before the sun, moon, and stars came into existence. They insist that the Creation happened just a few thousand years ago—not billions of years in the past, as science teaches.

The visitor who challenged me to debate holds a doctorate in physical education and is listed as "an adjunct professor of physiology for the Institute for Creation Research" at Santee, California. He implied that he's motivated only by scientific interest—but his group's Web site (www.icr.org) is that of a church. It proclaims:

> We believe God has raised up ICR to spearhead Biblical Christianity's defense against the godless dogma of evolutionary humanism. . . . ICR is funded by God's people . . . to proclaim God's truth about origins.

The Institute for Creation Research calls itself "a Christ-focused creation ministry." It says humans were made fully developed "in the six literal days of the creation week described in Genesis." It says this was a "relatively recent" event and that fossils were formed during Noah's flood.

It says anyone not saved "solely" by Jesus will "be consigned to the everlasting fire prepared for the devil and his angels." In other words, a billion Muslims, a billion Hindus, and hundreds of millions of Buddhists, Jews, Baha'is, Shintoists, and others, are doomed to fry forever, according to the ICR.

Well, all this is standard fundamentalism—but it isn't science, and it would be illegal to teach it in public-school science classes, especially in cosmopolitan schools containing Muslim, Jewish, Hindu, Buddhist, and Baha'i children. Maybe you can see why I chose not to debate this mentality.

Incidentally, the visiting professor offered $250,000 to anyone who can prove evolution. If this column wins the reward, I'll donate it to a real science institute.

21

THE GOD BIZ

Gospel fervor gleamed in three thousand faces at the $30 million city arena at Charleston, West Virginia. People around me, arms upraised, jerked in spasms as they loosed the unknown tongue: "Ala-ga-roosh-a-la. Dee-dee-dee-dee." A young woman beside me leaped and squealed. Others wiped tears, swaying and rocking.

Evangelist Ernest Angley from Akron, a squat dynamo in a toupee, evoked the passion like a symphony conductor building a crescendo. He chanted faster into the transmitting microphone concealed in his elegant three-piece suit. His voice boomed from huge banks of speakers on each side of the stage.

"You've got to have the old-time power at this final hour. How many want to be blessed during the Ernest Angley program?" All hands rose. "Just open up to God. Say, 'I'll take the anointing, Lord.' Say it: 'Lord!'"

Previously published in *Penthouse*, December 1980.

The crowd shouted, "LORD!"

"All of you that God has spoken to at some time, raise your hands." Two thousand hands went up. "See, we're not so crazy. We're in touch with heaven. It doesn't matter what people say, because we're on our way to heaven. The Lord's with us! The Lord's with us! Come on, everyone: The Lord's with us! The Lord's with us!"

The chant spread over the arena. Vaguely, I recalled *Gott Mit Uns* on Wehrmacht belt buckles.

While the fever was high, Angley launched a forty-minute collection: "Everyone say, 'Lord, tell me what to give in this offering tonight.' It's good to make a covenant with God. I'd rather give my money to God than to doctors and drugstores. I know there are some here who could make a $1,000 covenant, or $500. Don't be afraid. God will stand by you."

He asked a show of hands by all who would make a $100 covenant. Barely a dozen hands rose. He exhorted and pleaded: "Not a penny goes to me or the singers. It all goes for TV time. Your money will reach new souls. Through TV, I preach to more people every weekend than Christ did in his whole time on earth. Isn't that wonderful? And you're part of it. . . . Don't worry about your finances. Put it all in the hands of God."

Then he called for $50 covenants. About a hundred hands went up. "All right, everyone who can make a $25 covenant, stand up and say, 'Lord, I love you.' Stand up for Jesus. Stand and say, 'I love you, Jesus'. . . . Now $10 covenants: Stand up and say, 'I love Jesus. I love him. I love him. I love him.' . . . Now $5 covenants. . . ."

Finally, after all had stood, the stocky preacher told the crowd to sit and write checks to insert in envelopes that had been distributed. While the people wrote, Angley's gospel rock combo—with electric guitars, a trap set, and a grand piano—sang about going to heaven when the Rapture comes.

Afterward, the evangelist asked everyone to wave the filled envelopes over their heads. Then he called for a second offering of dollar bills to pay the $1,000 arena rent and stagehand cost. Angley asked everyone to wave envelopes in one hand and dollars in the other. An ocean of fluttering mammon engulfed us. Ushers gathered the money in buckets and took it to a locked room under the bleachers.

The show concluded with a healing line. A mother presented her brain-damaged little boy. The preacher seized him with a shrieking "Heeeaaalllll!!!" and then chortled: "He felt that, all right." Arthritic crones and hard-of-hearing laborers went through the line, many falling backward in a holy swoon when they were grabbed.

Angley also bestowed healing upon various cripples in wheel-chairs in the front row. After the service, relatives wheeled them away.

In the arena lobby, assistants sold Angley books and magazines containing endless testimonial letters from followers saying their cancers or diabetes or rheumatism or warts had vanished at the healer's touch. Angley's columns say that God gave him the power to "discern spirits," thus he can see ugly demons inside the ill. Like-wise, he says, he can see an angel beside him onstage at every arena, while other angels move through crowds, plucking out demons and curing ailments.

After the show, Angley's troupe boarded two vista-dome buses and two tractor-trailers for the next city and the next convention arena. On weekends the evangelist returns to his home base: a garish Akron cathedral that cost his followers $2.5 million. It has imported chandeliers, Italian statues, twenty-four-karat gold veneer on the pulpit and piano, a red-lit "fountain of blood," and side-by-side pic-tures of Angley and Jesus. The cathedral is dedicated to the healer's late wife, who died of ulcerative colitis despite his demon-extracting powers. Her tomb is under a twenty-three-foot-high, twenty-ton marble angel on the church lawn.

The day after the revival, as a newsman, I interviewed several people who had been healed onstage. A retired roofer with only four teeth claimed that he had been cured of hardening of the arteries, diabetes, and myriad other ailments. He lapsed into the unknown tongue while telling me about it. As for a deaf-mute young man, his mother said his condition was unchanged. A plump matron mistak-enly thought I worked for the Angley organization. She said her nerve and stomach trouble was improved, and "an inch-long thing that flopped in my ear is gone, praise the Lord!" She promised to begin mailing money soon. She asked if Angley's staff would pray for "my boy Jack, who has a demon in him." When I asked the nature of the demon, she said: "Well, Jack got sent back to prison because he couldn't stay out of fights while he was on parole."

That's one glimpse into the gospel gold mine that is producing billions—billions—of dollars for evangelists and their enterprises. Angley keeps his revenue tightly secret, but the scope of his national tours and hundred-station telecasts indicates a gross between $10 million and $20 million a year.

Here's a look down a different shaft of the gold mine.

A young Californian, Timothy Goodwin of Long Beach, was paralyzed in a car wreck that wasn't his fault. That was his first tragedy. His second was religious. He later filed a fraud suit telling this pathetic story.

He was convinced by leaders of "The Way" Bible society, a talking-in-tongues outfit, that his paralysis would be cured in a year if he moved to the sect's headquarters in Ohio and donated large sums from his accident settlement. He gave $210,000—and later paid $10,000 more for a Cadillac for a Way leader, $11,000 for a BMW auto for another Way chief, and $13,000 for extraneous gifts requested by Way officials. The healing didn't work, and Goodwin felt "took."

After he sued, The Way countersued him for slander. The case was settled out of court in secret, and the quadriplegic moved back to California. Goodwin's attorney told me that the sect refunded all of Goodwin's money on the condition that he never discuss the matter.

Another vein of the gold mine was worked by Bishop John W. Barber of Alabama, a dazzler who wore white tuxedos and drove luxury cars. He persuaded believers to buy $1,000 bonds in his Apostolic Faith Church of God Live Forever, Inc. Oldsters paid $100 down and sent installments to the Christian Credit Corporation of Nashville. His operation spread over eight states and then abruptly folded, and Barber moved to North Carolina. Lawyer Henry Haile of Nashville was appointed US receiver. Haile told me: "It's unbelievable. He sold $1.5 million in worthless bonds and also borrowed from twenty banks, but I can't imagine why anyone trusted him. He testified under oath he didn't file income tax returns for six years, yet he always had a new Lincoln and a big home."

The Ernest Angley television miracle crusade, The Way International, and the Apostolic Faith Church of God Live Forever, Inc., are three eddies in America's gospel flood.

Old-time magical religion has become a major cultural phenomenon in America. Celebrity evangelists in lavish hairdos have won followings that alarm mainline churches. The Gallup Poll says fifty million Americans now consider themselves "born again," and they shell out enough money to support a booming fundamentalist industry. Sales of gospel books, magazines, and records have soared past $1 billion a year. A million families have removed their children from public schools and pay for them to attend five thousand evangelical schools. A consortium of born-again businessmen has joined with the Campus Crusade for Christ to raise $1 billion for the world's biggest advertising campaign to prepare everyone for the Second Coming.

Revival tents of yesteryear are forgotten relics. Now the action is in astrodomes and multimillion-dollar megachurches with television studios. Fundamentalist "networks" keep broadcast dishes aimed at fixed-orbit satellites, bouncing programs over the continent twenty-four hours a day. Competing evangelists buy $600 million worth of radio and television time a year, paid for by their followers. At last count, the United States had fourteen-hundred all-gospel radio stations and about thirty gospel television stations, some operated by born-again folk, some run by shrewd businessmen who know where the money is.

The boom has political power. Coalitions try to mobilize fundamentalists into the nation's strongest voter bloc to pass "moral" laws and elect "moral" candidates, nearly all Republicans. Anita Bryant and revivalist Jerry Falwell launched a "Clean Up America" drive against pornography, abortion, and homosexuals.

Other gospel big guns summoned two hundred thousand born-again believers to a "Washington for Jesus" demonstration to back "pro-God" legislation. Evangelist Pat Robertson declared: "We have enough votes to run the country. And when the people say, 'We've had enough,' we are going to take over."

The gospel boom is under intense study by pundits. Author Jeremy Rifkin says it's "the single most important cultural force in American life" and might lead to fascism. Some sociologists think it's a backlash to the radicalism of the 1960s. Some say it's a breakaway from insipid conventional churches.

But one aspect has hardly been mentioned: rip-off. Part of the billion-dollar industry is cunning fraud, or bald opportunism, or exploitation of the superstitious, or tyrannical misuse of donated money by weirdo leaders. In my job as newspaperman and religion writer, I've covered the territory for many years and watched it grow.

While the born-again bandwagon gathered momentum, gospel scams and abuses surfaced with increasing frequency. For instance:

- Dapper Oklahoma evangelist James Roy Whitby was known in the gospel world for saving Anita Bryant when she was a Tulsa schoolgirl. But he was convicted of swindling an eighty-three-year-old religious widow out of $25,000. Then he was charged with selling $4 million in worthless Gospel Outreach bonds. Accused with him the second time were three convicted swindlers, including the Rev. Tillman Sherron Jackson of Los Angeles, who had previously bilked the born-again in the Baptist Foundation of America—a $26 million fraud that caused a congressional probe.

- Another big-money evangelist was Garner Ted Armstrong, whose national broadcasts drew $75 million a year to the Worldwide Church of God run by Garner and his father, Herbert W. Armstrong. Money poured in from followers, many of whom met in secret groups and donated 30 percent of their incomes. Garner lived like a maharaja in a California mansion with his own private jet, elegant sports cars—and, allegedly, female believers in bed. Trouble hit when some members published a protest. They accused Garner of sex and Herbert of self-enrichment. Chess champion Bobby Fischer said the elder Armstrong had used "mind control" to take nearly $100,000 from him. The father fired the son, who started a new television religion.

  California's attorney general filed a receivership suit accusing Herbert and church treasurer Stanley Rader of "pilfering" at least $1 million a year for themselves. Gold bullion owned by the sect was reported missing. Financial records indicated that Herbert and Rader each got salaries of $200,000 plus fabulous expense accounts. Garner accused Rader of taking $700,000 from the church in one year. Garner's sister said Rader had three homes, a horse stable, a

Maserati, a Mercedes, and a limousine. The US Supreme Court upheld the attorney general's right to investigate the church. Meanwhile, little is left of perhaps $1 billion of believers' money that was squandered over the years.

- Handsome, tuxedo-clad faith healer LeRoy Jenkins of South Carolina grossed $3 million a year by selling miracle water and prayer cloths and healing T-shirts to believers who watched him on sixty-seven television stations. He made an emergency appeal for $300,000 to pay church debts and then bought himself a $250,000 home two weeks later. He heavily insured a vacant cathedral just before it was hit by a mysterious explosion.

   Jenkins was sentenced to a twelve-year prison term for conspiring to (1) burn the home of a state trooper who had given his daughter a speeding ticket, (2) burn the home of a creditor, and (3) mug a journalist who had exposed his money abuses and drug arrests. Evidence came from a police undercover agent in the evangelist's staff. (The reporter, Rick Ricks, told me that police had warned him in advance he was to be "set up" by an anonymous telephone offer of information, so when the call came, he didn't go to meet the informant.) After Jenkins entered a South Carolina state prison, his staff distributed rerun tapes of his *Revival of America* show. For several months, the preacher still looked out of television screens around the United States and begged "love offerings," although he actually was in a cell.

- The whole world knows the story of the PTL Club of Charlotte, North Carolina, whose millionaire leader, evangelist Jim Bakker, went to prison for fraud and sex abuses. A Charlotte radio station mockingly advertised a "Pass the Loot" Club.

- Another such wipeout hit millionaire evangelist Jimmy Swaggart, who was caught soliciting prostitutes.

- The Rev. Hakeem Abdul Rasheed (alias Clifford Jones) and a young woman aide were convicted of mail fraud in California.

They had operated a $20-million-a-year church in an Oakland movie theater. Members who donated $500 became "ministers of increase." Then, periodically, the pastor called them forward to receive $2,000 "increases from God," while the congregation cheered. Bigger gifts drew bigger returns. Spreading excitement caused joiners to donate as much as $30,000 each. The church collected up to $350,000 a night. Rasheed/Jones had ankle-length mink coats, diamonds, a $100,000 Rolls-Royce, and a million-dollar yacht. His downfall came after he reported to police that four armed robbers took more than $300,000 from him aboard his hundred-foot boat, and detectives began wondering why a minister had so much money. It turned out that his church was a "Ponzi scheme" using new donations to pay former donors.

- The Rev. Robert Carr of Durham, North Carolina, was sentenced to ten years in prison for taking paychecks, food stamps, and welfare checks from members of his Church of God and True Holiness. He and other church leaders kept believers like slaves in a dormitory, forced them to work in a poultry plant, and pocketed their earnings. Carr's daughter and son-in-law also got prison terms, and a fourth church official became a fugitive.

- Bethesda Christian Center at Wenatchee, Washington—a gospel church, radio station, school, magazine publishing house, college, and gasoline station—was jolted when more than $1 million was reported missing and administrator James Eyre was jailed on embezzlement charges. About $340,000 that members lent to the church vanished. So did nearly $1 million that members put into deals such as diamond investments.

- American Consumer Inc. was indicted on one thousand counts of mail fraud for selling the "Cross of Lourdes" at $15.95 each, falsely claiming that the crosses had been dipped in France's miracle pool and blessed by the pope in Rome. The company was fined $25,000 and ordered to refund $103,000 to buyers.

- Frost Brothers Gospel Quartet of Columbus, Ohio, launched Consumer Companies of America, a twenty-state chain. Born-again families who paid $534 for orders of merchandise were entitled to enlist others and collect commissions on their orders. When enough were signed up, CCA was to build discount stores and give each member a share of the earnings. Evangelist Bob Harrington, "the chaplain of Bourbon Street," boosted the plan, saying, "God wants his people to succeed . . . and I thank God I'm identified with CCA." (I interviewed several CCA leaders—ex-gospel singers in flashy suits and high-rise hairdos.) The Frost Brothers lived like kings. President Alvin Frost bought a $1 million mansion. But they were convicted of stock violations, sued for fraud, slapped with a $370,000 tax lien, and charged with running a pyramid scheme. CCA collapsed in 1979 with losses for all.

- The Rev. Jerry Duckett of Williamson Church of God in West Virginia was indicted on charges of stealing $40,000 from his church's building fund. (His denominational superior swore out the embezzlement warrant and then was chagrined when I made the theft public.) Earlier, Duckett was fined $100 for pulling a pistol on a service station attendant who wouldn't put leaded gasoline into his unleaded-only car.

- Before the Rev. Jim Jones went entirely nuts, his People's Temple was a money machine. He required members to give 40 percent of their income and sign over their homes, insurance policies, savings accounts, welfare checks, and Social Security checks. To hook the credulous, he staged cancer cures, dramatically seizing the ill (stooges in disguise) and pulling out tumors (chicken gizzards). While his temple still was in San Francisco, two disillusioned members, Al and Jeanie Mills, led defectors in leaking to *New West* magazine that Jones's cures were fake and he was milking followers. After Jones moved to Guyana—and led nine hundred believers in the cyanide horror that stunned the world—troves of money were found. More than $7 million was discovered in two Panama banks, $3 million was in Guyana banks, and

$200,000 was in other Caribbean banks, while $700,000 cash and $2 million in real estate were still in California.

Rebels Al and Jeanie Mills started a refugee center for Jonestown survivors, amid reports that Jones had left behind a "hit squad" to kill defectors. The Millses published a book about the minister's abuses. Then the couple and their fifteen-year-old daughter were found executed, shot in the head.

- The Rev. Roland Gray of Bethel Missionary Baptist Church in Chicago was convicted of theft, fraud, and conspiracy. He reported his income was only $20 a week so he could falsely collect $43,000 in welfare checks and food stamps—while he concealed that he had $46,000 in cash, several luxury automobiles, expensive furs, and three homes. He also engaged in insurance fraud, collecting $56,000 from seventy-three bogus insurance claims. He got two years in prison.

- Marjoe Gortner, an aging boy evangelist, confessed that his exuberant revivals were a moneymaking fraud, carefully rehearsed and timed to suck big offerings from yokels. He said his parents pocketed $3 million from his boyhood tours. To expose the racket, Gortner made a documentary movie of himself fleecing congregations and gleefully counting piles of money in motel rooms, whooping, "Thank you, Jesus!" Gortner went on to be an actor, and fundamentalism went on unfazed.

- The Rev. DeVernon LeGrand, who headed St. John's Pentecostal Church of Our Lord in Brooklyn, recruited many teenage "nuns" who solicited money for his church. The pastor, age fifty, was convicted of raping one of the seventeen-year-old nuns. Then the bodies of two different nuns were found in a pond at LeGrand's farm in the Catskills. He and a son were convicted of murdering them. Finally, the pastor was found guilty of murdering his former wives.

- Bishop Lucius Cartwright and Pastor Albert Hamrick of St. Phillip's Pentecostal Church in Washington, DC, were sent to jail for embezzling $250,000 while administering food-stamp distribution. They used the money to buy a car, an ice cream parlor, and a bank building.

- A white revivalist, the Rev. James Eugene Ewing of Los Angeles, acquired thousands of black followers around the United States through an odd promise: If they sent him monthly donations, God would bless them with Cadillacs, color televisions, Mark IV Continentals, new homes, and so on. "God's Gold Book Plan for Financial Blessings," it was called. Those who mailed their Gold Book pledges faithfully could expect "power to get wealth," Ewing said. His monthly newsletter was filled with photos of pledge-payers beaming over new Eldorados or stereos. Followers were also urged to buy "miracle billfolds" and "golden horn-of-plenty neck charms." (An architect friend of mine sent a fake name to Ewing and collected his mailings to pass around the office as funny-sad reading.) The *Los Angeles Times* said Ewing grossed $4 million a year. *Newsweek* said he spent only 1 percent of it on charitable work. Even so, his church filed bankruptcy.

- The Children of God enlisted five thousand teenagers to testify for Jesus in city streets. Members were required to give the sect all their income for life. New York's attorney general issued a report accusing the group's leaders of fraud, tax evasion, and bizarre forced sex.

- Dr. Billy James Hargis was the king of the anti-Communist preachers after the McCarthy era. He denounced socialism, sex, and satanism—and drew millions from right-wing supporters. He lived in a $500,000 Tulsa mansion, had a farm in the Ozarks, and enjoyed the national spotlight. But he was ruined when *Time* magazine revealed that he sodomized male and female students at his tiny fundamentalist college. (The truth leaked out after Hargis performed a wedding of two students and on their honeymoon each told the other of going to bed with their spiritual leader.)

- The Rev. Guido John Carcich was convicted of embezzling $2.2 million from the Pallottine Fathers in Baltimore. The Catholic group collected $20 million in donations to help "the starving, sick, and naked," but only 3 percent of the money reached charitable work. Incoming contributions were handled at a secret warehouse, where Carcich told workers to throw away prayer-request letters unless they contained money. He was sentenced to a year of prison counseling work.

Ironically, victims of a gospel rip-off rarely realize that they're victims. They usually stay devoted to their preacher, no matter what, and view all accusations against him as tricks of the devil.

Redneck religion has always been part of America—since the Scopes "Monkey Trial" in Tennessee, since Carry Nation smashed the saloons, since Aimee Semple McPherson was buried with a live telephone in her ornate coffin in case God resurrected her. The United States always had scripture literalists obsessed with sin, one-preacher denominations, Pentecostals who spout "the tongues," faith healers who grab the lame, hillbilly congregations picking up rattlesnakes, Adventists who announce the end of the world, sex haters who burn books and rock albums, tabernacle-goers who "dance in the spirit" and writhe on the floor, and Bible prophecy fans who think that the Lost Tribes of Israel moved to England and became American settlers.

Why did they cease being a fringe and seize the foreground with such numbers and money? What caused the billion-dollar gospel boom? Much of it was created by three electronic marvels: (1) super-slick videotape production that gives a "class" look to television shows, (2) fixed-orbit satellites that relay broadcasts all over America for pickup by stations and cable systems, (3) computerized fund-raising centers able to receive millions of letters bearing $10 and $20 checks and to mail back machine-written responses selected by coding and disguised to appear personal.

As television's drawing power grew apparent, a crowd of celebrity preachers took to the air, competing for listener-donors. Today more than a thousand gospel shows are bounced off the satellites or distributed by radio tape and videotape to stations and cables. It's a bonanza for the broadcast industry. A typical clear-channel radio station, WWVA of Wheeling, sells $1 million worth of evening half hours to revivalists annually. Billy Graham pays up to $25,000 per television station per hour for his prime-time crusades.

Believers foot the bill. Most shows work like this: Watchers are invited to write for a gift, such as a four-cent "Jesus First" lapel pin. Once a viewer's name and address go into the computer, he gets letters urging him to become a "faith partner" and send monthly donations. The computer keeps track of big givers and little givers—and ejects names that don't produce after three mailings. (Some evangelists raise extra money by selling their donor lists to others.) Computers also dispatch monthly newsletters and sometimes choose prewritten replies to viewers who write about spiritual or personal problems.

The more magnetic a revivalist is, the more watcher-supporters he draws, which allows him to buy time on more stations, which draws more donors, which buys more air time, which draws more donors, and so on. His operation also can expand by the sale of books, records, magazines, gospel novelties, and tape cassettes.

America's evangelical bandwagon continues to roll, spanning all the way from born-again President Jimmy Carter to Manson cult killers Tex Watson and Susan Atkins, now saved and selling paperbacks about it. And the gospel gold mine continues to produce billion-dollar revenues, with no end in sight.

22

ADVENTURES IN THE BIBLE BELT

For many years in my West Virginia newspaper career, I was a religion reporter—and, believe me, I met some amazing denizens of Appalachia's Bible Belt.

One was Clarence "Tiz" Jones, the evangelist-burglar. He had been a state champion amateur boxer in his youth but succumbed to booze and evil companions and spent a hitch in prison. Then he was converted and became a popular Nazarene revivalist. He roved the state, drawing big crowds, with many coming forward to be saved.

But police noticed a pattern: In towns where Jones preached, burglaries happened. Eventually, officers charged him with a break-in. This caused a backlash among churches. Followers said Satan and his agents were framing the preacher. A "Justice for Tiz Jones" committee was formed. Protest marches were held.

Then Jones was nabbed red-handed in another burglary, and his guilt was clear. He went back to prison.

Previously published in the *Charleston Gazette*, December 7, 1993.

Another spectacular West Virginia minister was "Dr." Paul Collett, a faith healer who claimed he could resurrect the dead—if they hadn't been embalmed. Collett set up a big tent in Charleston and drew multitudes, including many in wheelchairs and on crutches. The healer said he had revived a corpse during a previous revival. He urged believers to bring him bodies of loved ones, before embalming.

Collett moved his show into an old movie theater and broadcast over radio stations. One night he said a cancer fell onto the stage. Another night, he said he turned water into wine.

I attended a service and wrote a skeptical account—focusing on his many money collections. After the article appeared, forty of Collett's followers invaded the newsroom. Luckily, it was my day off. The night city editor called police and summoned burly printers from the type shop, who backed the throng out the door.

Collett claimed to have ten-thousand adherents. For five years, he collected money to build a twelve-doored "Bible Church of All Nations," which was to be "the biggest tabernacle in West Virginia." Then he moved to Canada, leaving not a rack behind.

He returned some years later and preached at a serpent-handling church deep in the hills. (I often wrote about the ardent mountain worshipers who pick up buzzing rattlesnakes and thrust their hands into fire to show their faith. They're earnest and decent people— even though they have a high mortality rate during prayer services.)

The leader of the serpent church, Elzie Preast—who never took money from members—began to suspect that Dr. Collett was bilking his congregation. In an Old Testament–type showdown, the two ministers scuffled, one shouting "Manifest him, Lord!" and the other yelling "Rebuke the devil!"

Then Dr. Collett vanished for good. Meanwhile, the serpent churches spawned other tales.

Once a weekly newspaper printed a photo of a church wedding—and the bride and the groom each held a rattler.

Another time, politicians in a rural county allowed serpent-handlers to meet in the dilapidated courthouse. Some snakes escaped into crevices in the walls—and emerged weeks later, causing bedlam among courthouse employees.

A former University of Charleston sociologist, Dr. Nathan Gerrard, studied the serpent phenomenon. He administered a psychological test to a flock and gave the same test to a nearby Methodist congregation as a control group. The serpent handlers came out mentally healthier.

Once the great Harvard theologian Harvey Cox accompanied Dr. Gerrard and me to a different serpent church. When the worshipers began their trancelike "dancing in the spirit," we were surprised to see Dr. Cox leap up and join the hoofing.

Later, visiting professors accompanied us to a third serpent church. One professor's wife, barely five feet tall, was an opera soprano. The worshipers—whose music usually is the twang of electric guitars—asked her to sing. She stood on the altar rail and trilled "Musetta's Waltz" from *La Boheme* while the congregation listened respectfully.

Meanwhile, the parade of colorful evangelists never stopped. One was faith healer Henry Lacy, who handed out calling cards saying simply "Lacy the Stranger." He often came into the newsroom to lay hands on reporters to cure their hangovers. He once offered to halt a cold wave in West Virginia if state officials would return his driver's license, which had been confiscated.

And there was roving healer A. A. Allen, who visited West Virginia with jars containing froglike bodies that he said were demons he had cast out of the sick. He vanished after a revival at Wheeling and was found dead of alcoholism in a San Francisco hotel room with $2,300 in his pocket.

(Marjoe Gortner, the boy evangelist who later confessed that his show was a fraud, said Allen once advised him how to tell when a revival was finished and it was time to go to the next city: "When you can turn people on their head and shake them and no money falls out, then you know God's saying, 'Move on, son.'")

And "the Plastic Eye Miracle," the Rev. Ronald Coyne, visited Charleston. He was a one-eyed evangelist who said a faith healer had enabled him to see through his artificial eye. Several of us in the audience wrapped tape over his good eye, and he read items aloud, using his empty eye socket. I was mystified.

Those were heady days in the Bible Belt—before evangelists created million-dollar TV empires and became the ayatollahs of the Republican Party. The holy rovers of yesteryear provided marvelous theater. Today's mountain religion seems pale in comparison.

23

THE UNITARIAN QUANDARY

The largest identifiable body of agnostics in America is within the Unitarian Universalist Church, a traditional stronghold of freethinking. A 1987 survey found that only 3 percent of UUs believed in the standard supernatural God of conventional religion. Two-thirds acknowledged a life force or spirit of love—but 28 percent called the word God "an irrelevant concept."

More recently, in a 1997 survey of the denomination's 220,000 members, about half of respondents described themselves as humanists—by far the largest category. Doubt was strongest among older members. They're a remnant of a postwar heyday when multitudes of skeptical scientists and professors joined UU as a new Enlightenment. In those days, the denomination's Beacon Press printed hard-hitting critiques of religion, such as works of Paul Blanshard. Some churches displayed slogans such as "To Question Is the Answer" and a Peter Ustinov remark: "Beliefs are what divide people. Doubt unites them."

Previously published in *Free Inquiry*, Fall 2002.

Today, thousands of these UU secular humanists feel voiceless because their organization rarely questions the invisible spirits and magical heavens of major religions. Unitarian Universalism has grown so diverse—embracing Wicca priestesses, liberal Christians, Buddhist meditators, New Age mystics, postmodern symbolists, and so forth—that any official rationalist assertion would hurt someone's feelings. Questioning the supernatural is taboo. A polite silence prevails. Beacon Press now prints "uplift" books.

Worse, many ministers talk of God and Jesus in ways that boggle the agnostic majority. The denomination's president, once an avowed atheist, now chatters about God. He told a Massachusetts congregation: "The task of the Unitarian side of our faith is to find our own relationship to the divine, to God. The task of our Universalist side is to view that God as a loving God." After the September 11 religious horror, he reassured America: "There is a loving God who will hold out her hands to hold us . . . and be there to catch us as we fall."

We skeptics in the pews are mystified by such theism. In the past, UU took no stand on the existence, or nonexistence, of God. Now our national leader and numerous ministers are proclaiming the former, and we who lean toward the latter are left out in the cold.

At my UU fellowship in West Virginia, one minister (a once–Southern Baptist who had lost his faith) declared that God is the heart of the church. This caused turmoil, eventually followed by additional complications that produced his ouster and a bitter rift in the congregation.

"Spirituality" is today's UU buzzword, and it appeals to great numbers of new Unitarians. Wicca priestesses in my congregation talk of "the goddess" and "spirits of the north, south, east, and west." Being literal-minded, I ask what they mean—but I never understand the answers. The "women's spirituality" group in my church deals tarot cards (but ignores my suggestion of Ouija boards).

In 1997, the *New York Times* magazine printed a special issue on religious diversity in America. The UU example was a woman minister who heard a magical voice speak to her while she whirled in a spiral dance led by Starhawk, the witch. I was embarrassed to have my church represented by auditory hallucinations.

Doubters among Unitarians tend to gravitate to the church's

adult discussion circles, where they ponder physics, philosophy, psychology, social issues, and the like. Some of them don't attend the main "worship" services, which are replicas of hymn-singing Protestant rituals. Or if they attend, it's done partly like a family obligation to avoid ruffling feathers among fellow members.

Many of the skeptics join the UU humanist affiliate, or a small group called UU Infidels. Other sparks of the old freethinking remain. Recently, one of my minister friends spoke on "Why I Am an Agnostic" and "Why I Am an Existentialist." But he's an exception. Most congregations avoid such touchy topics.

So you see, perhaps a hundred thousand American agnostics belong to a movement that once was a pioneer in religious doubt, but now they feel marginalized within their own organization. They can't question the surrounding mysticism without seeming rude. I described this dilemma in an article for the official UU magazine, but it was rejected. (I understood. Naturally, the "house organ" must promote harmony within the ranks, not sow discord.)

However, I think those hundred thousand UU skeptics at least should discuss their predicament. Knowing that many agnostic Unitarians also read *Free Inquiry*, I want to share the essay that *UUWorld* wouldn't print. Here it is.

*   *   *

A great truth about our denomination rarely is mentioned. It isn't cited in our Seven Principles or other church declarations. Yet it lies at the heart of our movement.

This unspoken truth is that most UUs doubt the supernatural. We question the mystical, magical, miracle claims central to all other faiths: the pantheon of gods, devils, heavens, hells, saviors, angels and the rest. In fact, disbelief is the foremost feature setting UU apart from conventional religions. UU is the only church that welcomes complete atheists as members.

If doubt is entwined in our church, why the silence about it? After all, it has been crucial, right from the beginning. The very word "unitarian" conveys disbelief. While Christianity proclaims three invisible deities in the Trinity (and additional spirits such as Satan, the Virgin Mary, demons, angels, saints, etc.), early Unitarians doubted that

Jesus was a god and said so. They were called anti-trinitarians—
doubters of the Trinity. Some pioneers, such as physician Michael
Servetus, were put to death for it. The first known Unitarian preacher,
Francis David of Transylvania, was imprisoned for his doubts and
died in a cell. The English home and laboratory of scientist-Unitarian
Joseph Priestley were burned by a Christian mob.

In America, renowned Unitarians were skeptics. Although Thomas
Jefferson never officially quit the Anglican Church, he's somewhat our
patron saint. We all know that he wrote, wishfully: "I trust there is not
a young man now living in the United States who will not die a Unitarian" (letter to Dr. Benjamin Waterhouse, June 26, 1822).

But we are less aware of his contempt for Christian supernaturalism and the ministers who preached it: "Question with boldness
even the existence of a God; because, if there be one, he must more
approve of the homage of reason than that of blindfolded fear"
(letter to his nephew, Peter Carr, August 10, 1787).

"To talk of immaterial existences is to talk of nothings. To say
that the human soul, angels, god, are immaterial, is to say that they
are nothings, or that there is no god, no angels, no soul. I cannot
reason otherwise" (letter to John Adams, August 15, 1820).

"The priests of the different religious sects . . . dread the advance
of science as witches do the approach of daylight" (letter to Correa
de Serra, April 11, 1820).

The first Unitarian president, John Adams, was less abrasive than
Jefferson, yet time after time he scorned established churches. He
signed a 1797 treaty with Tripoli declaring that "the government of
the United States is not, in any sense, founded on the Christian religion." In an 1814 letter to John Taylor, he wrote:

> The priesthood have, in all ancient nations, nearly monopolized
> learning. . . . And, even since the Reformation, when or where has
> existed a Protestant or dissenting sect who would tolerate A FREE
> INQUIRY? [his capitals] The blackest billingsgate, the most
> ungentlemanly insolence, the most yahooish brutality is patiently
> endured, countenanced, propagated, and applauded. But touch a
> solemn truth in collision with a dogma of a sect, though capable
> of the clearest proof, and you will soon find you have disturbed a
> nest, and the hornets will swarm about your legs and hands, and
> fly into your face and eyes.

Unitarian minister Ralph Waldo Emerson wrote scornfully: "As men's prayers are a disease of the will, so are their creeds a disease of the intellect" ("Self-reliance," 1841). And he said: "Other world? There is no other world! Here or nowhere is the whole fact" (quoted by George Seldes in *The Great Quotations*).

Henry David Thoreau, another Unitarian (who, like Emerson, eventually quit churches entirely), sneered at religion as "a baby-house made of blocks" and wrote: "I did not see why the school-master should be taxed to support the priest, and not the priest the schoolmaster" (both from "On the Duty of Civil Disobedience," 1841).

This skeptic pattern continued through succeeding generations. Another Unitarian president, William Howard Taft (1857–1930), was offered the presidency of Yale University, at that time allied with the Congregationalist Church, but he declined on doctrinal grounds, saying he doubted the divinity of Christ.

Doubt of supernatural Christian beliefs was the driving force of the entire Unitarian movement in Europe and America. The rise of scientific thinking two centuries ago impelled many New England congregations to leave their former denominations and join the Unitarian tide.

Our chief distinguishing feature is the lack of a creed—which, indirectly, proves that UU is skeptical. Unlike standard churches, we don't chant that we "believe in God, the Father almighty, creator of heaven and earth" and his "only begotten son," and so on because we cannot. Many freethinking members would recoil and rebel.

Today, however, it seems taboo for any UU to voice the skepticism that lies at the core of our church. In my half century of affiliation, I've rarely heard clear assertions of disbelief in the aforementioned gods, devils, heavens, hells, saviors, angels, and the rest. I haven't heard bold statements like those of Jefferson, Adams, Emerson, Thoreau, or Taft.

Worse, it has become fashionable for UU ministers and leaders to invoke God. Many of us in the pews can't guess what they're talking about. Obviously, they don't mean the god of evangelist Jerry Falwell, of President George W. Bush, or of Muslim terrorist Osama bin Laden. We assume they're speaking in theological crypto-jargon, with some abstruse, allegorical, postmodern meaning that's actually meaningless. Perhaps the denomination should require ministers who use the word to provide a definition.

Why does our denomination, rooted in doubt, never mention doubt—and even make standard-sounding appeals to God? Maybe it's because UU is so diversified. Questioning the supernatural might seem rude to members with New Age, Buddhist, Earth-centered, Christian, and other spiritual inclinations. Since UU takes a hands-off approach, with no creed, the church is open to a remarkable variety of people. Therefore, the only way to maintain harmony evidently is to avoid mentioning beliefs—even the skeptic beliefs that created the denomination.

Well, I don't want to hurt anyone's feelings, but I think we agnostics should be allowed to express our honest views within our church. I'd like to penetrate the silence but do it without injury. I wish the Unitarian Universalist Association could openly acknowledge its hands-off stance, with an official statement saying something like: "The UUA takes no position on the existence, or nonexistence, or God. Members are free to reach their own conclusions on this profound topic." Such a statement merely would express the reality that already exists—and it would show the world that UU is radically different from all other churches.

Every denomination provides fellowship, the nurturing "extended family" in which members share the joys and the problems of their lives. In this regard, UU is no different from the rest.

Every denomination advocates humanitarian social action to help the poor, the sick, the impaired, the old, and others in need. In this regard, UU is no different from the rest.

We're different in only one way: Unitarian Universalists doubt the magic claims of conventional religion. I wish we were allowed to say so.

24

THREE LITTLE WORDS: I DON'T KNOW

When I was a young reporter, I hung out with my newspaper buddies in all-night diners (liquor clubs were illegal in those days), earnestly debating the meaning of life.

Some of us couldn't swallow the standard explanation—that the purpose of life is to be saved by an invisible Jesus and go to an invisible heaven—but we couldn't see any alternatives that made sense.

One day I asked my city editor, an iconoclastic disciple of H. L. Mencken, how an honest person can answer the ultimate questions: Is there life after death? Is there a spirit realm of unseen gods and devils, heavens and hells? Is there a divine force running the universe? Since there's no tangible evidence, one way or the other, how can you make a sincere answer?

He replied: "You can say, 'I don't know.'"

That rang a bell in my mind. I suppose I had half-known it all

Delivered as a lecture at Marshall University and published in *UU Infidels Newsletter*, Autumn 2004.

along, in my confused search for answers, but now I saw clearly how to be truthful and straightforward about an extremely touchy, emotional subject. I felt liberated because it gave me a way to maintain integrity. Saying "I don't know" isn't really an answer, but it's the only answer I could give without lying or guessing or pretending.

Of course, those were the naive days of youth. I hadn't yet learned of a thousand philosophers who sweated through the same dilemma and reached the same conclusion. But it became a foundation stone of my psyche, never to leave me.

Once you say "I don't know," you're in conflict with the majority culture. All the supernatural religions and ministers claim that they do know. They say absolutely that invisible spirits exist. Hundreds of millions of Americans go to churches and pray to the unseen beings. Successful politicians always invoke the deities. When you say, "I don't know," you're clashing with all these people who claim to know.

It puts you out of step with the world—but I don't think a truthful person can take any other stance. From my viewpoint, the only honest mind is the unsure mind, the doubtful mind. It's the only outlook that doesn't claim knowledge that nobody actually possesses. This is the agnostic, skeptical, rationalist, scientific posture. To me, anything else is dishonest because it requires people to swear they know things they really don't.

To me, priests and theologians are lying when they declare that supernatural beings are real, that people are rewarded or punished after death. It isn't dishonest to speculate about such ideas—but the clergymen flatly say spirits exist, and pray to them, and even claim to know how the spirits want us to behave. That's absurd.

As Voltaire said, "Doubt is not a pleasant condition, but certainty is a ridiculous one."

Once you've crossed the "I don't know" threshold, maybe you'll take some logical steps that lead you further, beyond just a neutral, hands-off position. If you're scientific-minded, always looking for trustworthy evidence, you'll see that there isn't a shred of reliable proof for mystical, magical, miraculous things.

What's the evidence for an invisible heaven or hell? For invisible deities and devils? None, except ancient tribal writings and the pronouncements of priests. It's rather like the evidence for witches, ghosts, vampires, fairies, werewolves, demons, leprechauns, and others. Educated people know that the latter spooks are just imaginary.

By the time you reach this point, you may be pretty much convinced that the mystical beings worshiped by religions are just imaginary, too—that the whole rigmarole is a gigantic, worldwide, billion-member, trillion-dollar fantasy, a universal human delusion and self-deception that has been going on for ten thousand years.

And you may extend your skepticism to other fantastic things: astrology horoscopes, UFO abductions, seances with the dead, Ouija boards, New Age "channeling" of spirits, psychic prophecies, palm-reading, "dowsing" rods, and so on.

See how far you can be led by three little words: "I don't know."

If you proceed along this mental path, as I did, you'll face a tough decision: whether to dispute the True Believers you encounter or whether to stay silent.

There's little point in arguing with worshipers. They often become angry when challenged. (Bertrand Russell said it's because they subconsciously realize their beliefs are irrational—so they can't tolerate having them questioned.)

Time after time, I vow to avoid theological quarrels. But when an ardent believer tells me that God wants us to punish homosexuals, that prayer cures cancer, that Jesus opposes birth control, or that God disapproves of nudity and sex, I can't restrain myself. I don't want to be a religion basher, yet I turn into one.

Perhaps we unsure people should take a pledge: When believers confront us with dogmatic declarations about miraculous things, we will just smile sweetly and say, "I don't know."

CONCLUSION

The purpose of this book has been to present a variety of arguments against America's excessive religiosity and supernatural thinking—and to oppose the fundamentalist political forces wielding enormous power in the twenty-first century, marginalizing nonconformist, freethinking Americans.

The best safeguard against currents of oppressive theocracy lies in America's rising secularism. When large numbers of people renounce churches, diversity and democracy are protected. It becomes more difficult for strident believers to impose their taboos and rules on the whole culture.

Helping America follow the path of Europe into the Secular Age is a noble cause. Several bold thinkers have fought hard to advance scientific, humanistic thinking as an antidote for mysticism. Isaac

---

Adapted from a book review on Sagan's *The Demon-Haunted World*. Previously published in the *Charleston Gazette*, April 12, 1996, and syndicated nationally, and in *Free Inquiry*, Spring 1997.

Asimov, Paul Kurtz, Richard Dawkins, and many others have struggled in this effort.

One outstanding crusader was the late astronomer Carl Sagan, who was perhaps the world's most popular scientist during his time. Just before his death in 1996, he wrote a blunt attack on all forms of magical thinking. His book, *The Demon-Haunted World: Science as a Candle in the Dark*, assailed astrology horoscopes, faith healing, UFO "abductions," religious miracles, New Age occultism, fundamentalist "creationism," tarot-card reading, prayer, prophecy, palmistry, transcendental meditation, satanism, weeping statues, "channeling" of voices from the dead, holy apparitions, extrasensory perception, belief in life after death, "dowsing," demonic possession, the "supernatural powers" of crystals and pyramids, "psychic phenomena," and the like.

The book's message may be summed up: Many people believe almost anything they're told, with no evidence, which makes them vulnerable to charlatans, crackpots, and superstition. Only the scientific outlook, mixing skepticism and wonder, can give people a trustworthy grasp of reality. Sagan scorned supernatural aspects of religion. Here are some of his comments:

"If some good evidence for life after death were announced, I'd be eager to examine it; but it would have to be real scientific data, not mere anecdote. . . . Better the hard truth, I say, than the comforting fantasy."

"If you want to save your child from polio, you can pray or you can inoculate. . . . Try science."

"Think of how many religions attempt to validate themselves with prophecy. Think of how many people rely on these prophecies, however vague, however unfulfilled, to support or prop up their beliefs. Yet has there ever been a religion with the prophetic accuracy and reliability of science? . . . No other human institution comes close."

"Since World War II, Japan has spawned enormous numbers of new religions featuring the supernatural. . . . In Thailand, diseases are treated with pills manufactured from pulverized sacred Scripture. 'Witches' are today being burned in South Africa. . . . The worldwide TM [Transcendental Meditation] organization has an estimated valuation of $3 billion. For a fee, they promise through meditation to be able to walk you through walls, to make you invisible, to enable you to fly."

"The so-called Shroud of Turin . . . is now suggested by carbon-14 dating to be not the death shroud of Jesus, but a pious hoax from the 14th century—a time when the manufacture of fraudulent religious relics was a thriving and profitable home handicraft industry."[1]

Sagan quoted the Roman philosopher Lucretius: "Nature . . . is seen to do all things spontaneously of herself, without the meddling of the gods."[2]

And he quoted the Roman historian Polybius as saying the masses can be unruly, so "they must be filled with fears to keep them in order. The ancients did well, therefore, to invent gods and the belief in punishment after death."[3]

Sagan recounted how the medieval church tortured and burned thousands of women on absurd charges that they were witches. He said that "this legally and morally sanctioned mass murder" was advocated by great church fathers. "Inquisitional torture was not abolished in the Catholic Church until 1816," he wrote. "The last bastion of support for the reality of witchcraft and the necessity of punishment has been the Christian churches."[4]

The astronomer-author was equally scornful of New Age gurus, flying saucer buffs, seance "channelers," and others who tout mysterious beliefs without evidence. He denounced the tendency among some groups, chiefly fundamentalists and marginal psychologists, to induce people falsely to "remember" satanic rituals they experienced as children.

Again and again, Sagan said that wonders revealed by science are more awesome than any claims by mystics. He called children "natural scientists" because they incessantly ask "Why is the moon round?" or "Why do we have toes?" or the like. He urged that youngsters be inculcated with the scientific spirit of searching for trustworthy evidence.

Sagan's book, written late in his brief life, was more confrontational than his previous works. Perhaps, like Voltaire, he felt spurred by advancing age to take a stronger public stand against mysticism. It's a shame that America and the world lost this intensely honest advocate of truth.

Meanwhile, many others are continuing the struggle to loosen the grip of supernaturalism and hasten America's advance away from "the demon-haunted world." Each step means progress for humanity.

NOTES

1. Carl Sagan, *The Demon-Haunted World: Science as a Candle in the Dark* (New York: Random House, 1995), pp. 204, 30 (two on this page), 16, and 46 (in order of appearance).
2. Ibid., p. 310.
3. Ibid., p. 213.
4. Ibid., p. 413.